The 500 Hidden Secrets of

BARCELONA

INTRODUCTION

This is a guide to the Barcelona that almost no one knows. It takes you off the beaten track to discover the city's hidden gardens, little-known museums and best tapas bars. In these pages you will find the 5 most delicious seafood and fish restaurants, the 5 indispensable Gaudí creations and the 5 oldest and most charming stores in town.

You will discover the city's history but also its present. Barcelona is overwhelmingly alive, with daring new architecture, experimental cuisine, vibrant shopping areas and some of the best dance clubs in Europe.

This book was written with the ambition to escape the tourist-saturated areas and get the total Barcelona experience. So while there is room for Camp Nou, Barça's famous soccer arena in the Les Corts district, you'll also find 5 other reasons to visit this district. We'd like to think that this book suggests exciting ways to spend your Saturday night, as well as guide you towards the best brunch places and beautiful parks to enjoy the day after. To top it off, we added plenty of wild cards, like the 5 phrases you should know in Catalan, the 5 types of coffee you'll want to try and 5 reasons to look up in the street.

The 500 Hidden Secrets of Barcelona doesn't mention everything there is to see. There are already enough guide books and websites that cover the familiar sights. This is rather an intimate guide to the places the author would recommend to a friend who wants to discover the real Barcelona.

HOW TO USE
THIS BOOK?

This book lists 500 things you need to know about Barcelona in 100 different categories. Most of these are places to visit, with practical information like the address and sometimes the opening hours. Others are bits of information that help you get to know the city and its habitants. The purpose of this guide is to inspire you to explore the city, but it does not cover every aspect from A to Z.

The places listed in the guide are given an address (in which 'C/' is short for 'Carrer'), including the district, and a number. The district and number allow you to find the locations on the maps at the beginning of the book: first look for the map of the corresponding district, then look for the right number. A word of caution however: these maps are not detailed enough to allow you to locate specific places in the city. They are included to give you a sense of where things are, and whether they are close by other places of interest. You can obtain an excellent map in most hotels and at the Barcelona Tourist Information office, Plaça de Catalunya 17. Or the addresses can be located on a smartphone.

Please also bear in mind that cities change all the time. The chef who hits a high note one day, may be uninspiring on the day you happen to visit. The hotel ecstatically reviewed in this book might suddenly go downhill under a new manager. The bar considered one of the 5 coolest music clubs might be empty on the night you visit. This is obviously a highly personal selection. You might not always agree with it. If you want to leave a comment, recommend a bar or reveal your favourite secret place, you can contact the publisher at info@lusterweb.com or post a message on the author's blog *http://markcloostermans.blogspot.com*. Or follow *@500hiddensecrets* on Instagram and leave a comment – you'll also find free tips and the latest news about the series there.

THE AUTHOR

Mark Cloostermans (1977) studied English and Dutch literature before becoming a journalist and book critic for the Flemish daily newspaper *De Standaard*. In 2008 he visited Barcelona for the first time and fell in love instantly with the city's vibe and colours. He came back one year later and settled there in 2010.

Cloostermans blogs about literature, gastronomy and Barcelona on *http://markcloostermans.blogspot.com*. He recently published a book on the Belgian crime writer Georges Simenon (*De man die van vrouwen hield*) and is currently working on a collection of essays on TV-series and literature.

In drawing up the list of 500 hidden secrets of Barcelona, the author was helped by Isabelle Kliger (do find and follow her on Instagram!), Sandra Cloostermans, Jairo Guerrero and several locals. He also wishes to thank Bart Van Aken (for bringing him in contact with the publisher of this book), Tino van den Berg (for perfectly capturing the city in pictures) and Dettie Luyten (the editor, whose patience he tested on numerous occasions).

BARCELONA

overview

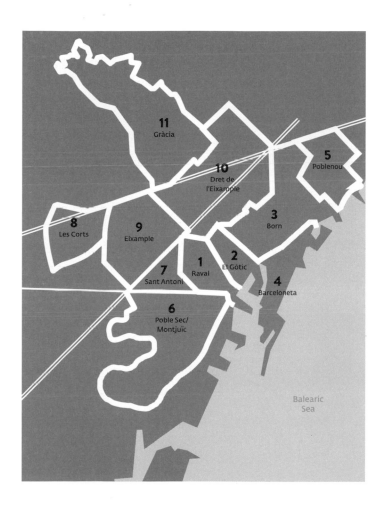

Map 1
RAVAL

Map 2
EL GÒTIC

Map 3

BORN

Map 4
BARCELONETA

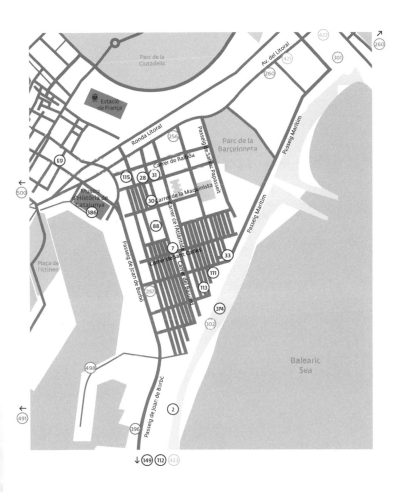

Map 5
POBLENOU

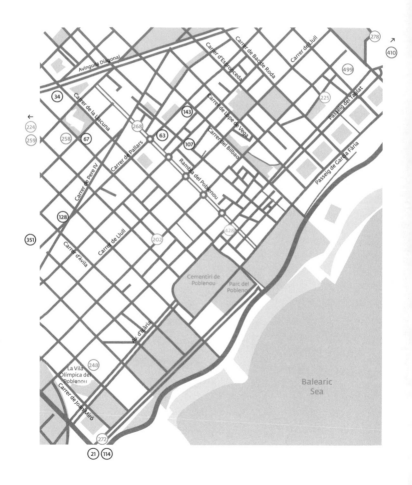

Map 6
POBLE SEC / MONTJUÏC

Map 7
SANT ANTONI

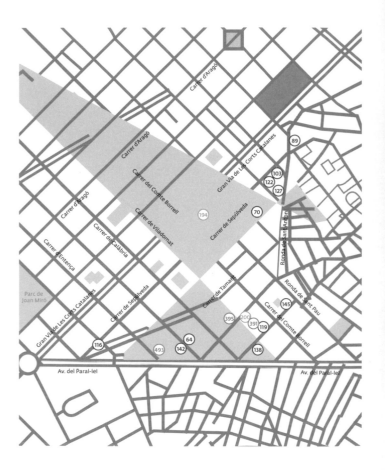

Map 8
LES CORTS

Map 9
EIXAMPLE

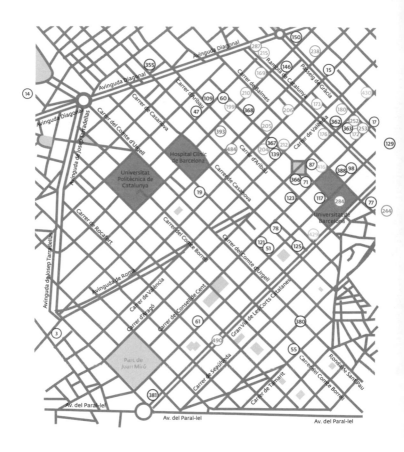

Map 10

DRET DE L'EIXAMPLE

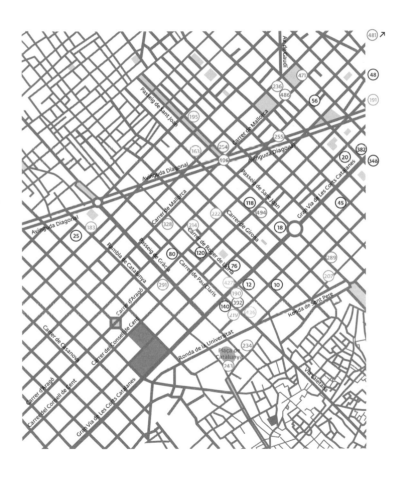

Map 11
GRÀCIA

EL CASAL

90 PLACES TO EAT OR BUY GOOD FOOD

---

5 restaurants with a

BREATHTAKING VIEW

---

1 MARTINEZ
Carretera de
Miramar 38
Poble Sec/Montjuïc ⑥
+34 (0)93 106 60 52
*www.martinez
barcelona.com*

Quite a good seafood restaurant,
although you really come here for the
view: it's high up on Montjuïc and
overlooks a large part of the city. The
ideal place for a romantic evening.

**2 RESTAURANT
OF THE CLUB
NATACIÓ ATLÈTIC-
BARCELONETA**
Plaça del Mar s/n
Barceloneta ④
+34 (0)93 221 00 10
www.cnab.cat

Overlooking the beach without being
overpriced, the restaurant on the ground
floor of this gym serves a great lunch,
with an emphasis on fish. Recently a
new restaurant opened right next to it:
Beach Garden. It's even closer to the sea,
but lacks the down-to-earth Barcelona
feel of the Club's restaurant.

3 VISUAL – GRAN HOTEL
TORRE CATALUNYA
Avinguda de Roma 2
Eixample ⑨
+34 (0)93 600 69 96
*www.torrecatalunya.
expohotels.com*

You wouldn't expect a place this nice
in this part of the city. After all, the
area around Sants railway station is
more highway than city. But up there
in Catalunya Tower is a restaurant with
classic Catalan cuisine and a 360-degree
view of the city. Awesome.

4 **B-LOUNGE RESTAURANT**
Rambla del Raval 17
Raval ⓘ
+34 (0)93 320 14 90
www.barcelo.com/es/raval/

This pretty swanky restaurant is part of the Barceló Raval Hotel and boasts a 360-degree terrace. The food is fine, decently priced and you get a wonderful view of one of Barcelona's busiest, most colourful neighbourhoods.

5 **MIRABLAU**
Plaça del Doctor Andreu s/n
Gràcia ⑪
+34 (0)93 418 58 79
www.mirablaubcn.com

If you take the Tramvia Blau up Tibidabo hill, this restaurant is where the tram will drop you off. The restaurant faces the sea. Needless to say the view (the city, Sagrada Familia, the sea, Montjuïc...) never gets dull. Mainly tapas, with a slightly adventurous touch.

1 MARTINEZ

5 great places to
EAT WITH THE LOCALS

---

6 **CAN EUSEBIO**
   C/ de Vila i Vilà 84
   Poble Sec/Montjuïc ⑥
   +34 (0)93 442 03 07

A couple of years ago, Poble Sec was 'rediscovered' by the people of Barcelona. This neighbourhood in between Raval and Montjuïc hill is lively without the messiness of Raval, and is certainly cheaper than tourist-heavy areas like Born. Can Eusebio is a case in point: very good tapas for next to nothing. Seven euros for dinner, two euros for dessert? Hard to beat.

7 **LA COVA FUMADA**
   C/ del Baluard 56
   Barceloneta ④
   +34 (0)93 221 40 61

An old-fashioned bodega, family-run and very popular with the Barcelona locals. The menu couldn't be more Mediterranean: marinated sardines, chickpeas with *morcilla* (black pudding) and the like.

8 **PIM PAM PLATS**
   Carrer del Rec 18
   Born ③
   +34 (0)93 315 20 93
   www.pimpamplats.com

Going for a night out? Then this is where to go for quick and hearty food that will get you through the night. Sit at a table at Pim Pam Plats and enjoy the staples of Italian cuisine, or go for a fine hamburger to the cheaper-looking little brother Pim Pam Burger, just around the corner.

9 QUIMET D'HORTA

Plaça d'Eivissa 10
Gràcia ⑪
+34 (0)93 358 19 16
www.quimethorta.com

The owners of Quimet d'Horta think big. The wall of bottles behind the counter: big. The number of sandwiches they serve: impressive. They have 85 different *bocadillos* (sandwiches) plus 37 types of tortillas on the menu. The ideal place to end your visit to the quiet Horta neighbourhood.

10 CASA FREIXO

Rambla Bruc 36
Dret de l'Eixample ⑩
+34 (0)93 302 20 89

This family-friendly Galician restaurant is filled with regulars at lunchtime. The lunch menu is nice indeed but we recommend coming back for dinner; especially their veal entrecote is delicious. And since Galicia lies at the coast (in the northwest of Spain), they also serve very good oysters and barnacles.

Our 5 favourite
MICHELIN STAR
RESTAURANTS

---

11 **SANT PAU**
Carrer Nou 10
Sant Pol de Mar
+34 (0)93 760 06 62
www.ruscalleda.com

There are two good reasons to hop on a train and visit nearby Sant Pol de Mar. One: the beach here is prettier and less crowded than in Barcelona. Two: this three-Michelin-star restaurant with chef Carme Ruscalleda. Original creations, local products and a magnificent setting make for a joyful dining experience.

12 **CAELIS**
Gran Via de les Corts
Catalanes 668
Dret de l'Eixample ⑩
+34 (0)93 510 12 05
www.caelis.com

A tasting menu for 80 euros will seem expensive to some, but Caelis (one Michelin star) is certainly not overcharging. Caviar, foie gras, beef tartar, tournedos Rossini and a Cristal Melba for dessert? Eating at Caelis is like cruising past the highlights of culinary history.

13 TICKETS

Avinguda del
Paral-lel 164
Poble Sec/Montjuïc ⑥
+34 (0)93 292 42 54
www.ticketsbar.es

Tickets is owned by Albert Adrià (of El Bulli fame), so expect playful dishes of tapas-size, exploring all the senses. Getting a table at Tickets is tough; make your reservation online two months beforehand. Once you're in, things get a lot easier: the waiter will ask what kind of food you like and will make the decisions for you.

14 VIA VENETO

C/ de Ganduxer 10
Eixample ⑨
+34 (0)93 200 72 44
www.viaveneto.es

A staple of Spanish haute cuisine, Via Veneto (one Michelin star) is a lavish-looking place. Try the red mullets with *sanfaina* (a stew of eggplant, tomato and onion) or the scorched rice with eel from the Catalonian delta (in the south of the region; very much worth a visit). This place is so firmly rooted in Catalan culinary history that it has become a reference itself.

15 LASARTE

C/ de Mallorca 259
Eixample ⑨
+34 (0)93 445 32 42
www.restaurantlasarte.
com

Exquisite-looking, exquisite-tasting dishes by chef Martín Berasategui, in a bright and spacious setting. Expensive, but also the kind of place (with two Michelin stars) you'll visit once in a lifetime, then talk about for years.

5 places to try
EXPERIMENTAL CUISINE

---

16 **ABAC**
Avinguda del Tibidabo 1
Gràcia ⑪
+34 (0)93 319 66 00
www.abacbarcelona.com

Jordi Cruz is one of Spain's most successful young chefs. This restaurant, embedded in the ABaC Hotel, specialises in surprises: daring combinations and dishes you could never imagine. The smoked beef tartar is already famous.

17 **MOMENTS**
Passeig de Gràcia 38
Eixample ⑨
+34 (0)93 151 87 81
www.mandarinoriental. com

Managed by Carme Ruscalleda and her son Raül Balam, Moments serves imaginative dishes in a theatre-like setting. You can watch the staff at work through the amber-tinted window in the back.

18 **GELONCH**
Carrer de Bailèn 56
Dret de l'Eixample ⑩
+34 (0)93 265 82 98
www.restaurunt gelonch.es

Gelonch is another restaurant that uses the latest technology to tease the taste out of food you only thought you knew. Seafood cannelloni, cod with almond cream, or traditional *crema catalana* with a sour apple sorbet… – there's very little *not* to recommend here.

19 DISFRUTAR

C/ de Villarroel 163
Eixample ⑨
+34 (0)93 348 68 96
*www.disfrutarbarcelona.
com*

The cosy bar near the entrance, the middle part where you can see the kitchen, or the beautiful terrace area in the back? No matter where you sit, the food here is always stunning, and the service is impeccable, warm and welcoming. The design of the restaurant, with a bright seventies-feel, mirrors the style of the Mercat del Ninot on the other side of the street.

20 MANAIRÓ

C/ de la Diputació 424
Dret de l'Eixample ⑩
+34 (0)93 231 00 57
www.manairo.com

Former bullring Monumental is just around the corner, which is appropriate for a meat restaurant that promises to use the entire animal in its dishes, snout to tail. Jordi Herrera's Manairó has a meat-heavy menu; even if there's fish on your plate, it's probably in combination with meat. The result is a pleasure for the eye and the palate.

5 exceptionally
STYLISH
RESTAURANTS

---

21 **ENOTECA**

C/ de la Marina 19-21
Poblenou ⑤
+34 (0)93 221 10 00
www.hotelartsbarcelona.
com/en/Dining/Enoteca

You won't stroll through the doors of Enoteca by chance. The restaurant is part of Hotel Arts, one of the two skyscrapers by the Barcelona beach. Here you'll not only find the perhaps most extensive wine list (700 bottles) of Barcelona, but also the amazing cuisine of Chef Paco Perez, who works with quality ingredients and morphs them into new creations.

22 **LLAMBER**

**Carrer de la Fusina 5
Born** ③
+34 (0)93 319 62 50
www.llamber.com

A *gastrotaverna* paradoxically combining wood panelling with a slightly industrial feel, and a place to be seen. It is in the heart of upmarket Born, right next to the recently renovated Mercat del Born, with Oriol Balaguer's fêted pastry store La Xocolateria as a neighbour.

23 **FONDA ESPAÑA**

C/ de Sant Pau 9-11
Raval ①
+34 (0)93 550 00 00
*www.hotelespanya.com/
es/restaurante-fonda-
espana/*

Architect Lluís Domènech i Montaner, creator of marvels such as the Hospital de Sant Pau and the Palau de la Música, designed the dining room of Hotel España, and it's simply stunning. The kitchen of chef German Espinosa does the location more than justice.

24 **7 PORTES**

Passeig Isabel II 14
Born ③
+34 (0)93 319 30 33
www.7portes.com

'Seven doors' give access to as many dining salons, all with a 19th-century feel. Even the waiters, with their long aprons, give the impression of having been there at least a century. The dishes are more than okay: classic Catalan cuisine in generous portions. In a neighbourhood full of tourist traps, it's a relief to find something as dependable as 7 Portes.

25 **WINDSOR**

C/ de Corsèga 286
Dret de l'Eixample ⑩
+34 (0)93 237 75 88
www.restaurant windsor.com

Windsor, taking up the entire ground floor of the building, is divided in separate spaces, some small and private, some bigger and more opulent. During lunch it attracts businessmen, in the evening people who like the waiters' hands-on approach and the excellent, classic but classy food. Windsor knows how to handle tradition.

5 delicious
FISH RESTAURANTS

---

26 CAL PEP
Plaça de les Olles 8
Born ③
+34 (0)93 310 79 61
www.calpep.com

Cal Pep is Catalan and means 'At Pep's', Pep being Josep Manubens Figueres, one of Catalonia's most famous chefs. The specialty here is fresh seafood, served tapas-style. Queue outside to get in for lunch, then sit at the bar. Great food, relaxed atmosphere.

27 DOS PALILLOS
Carrer d'Elisabets 9
Raval ①
+34 (0)93 304 05 13
www.dospalillos.com

Pricey, but no doubt one of the best seafood restaurants in town. All customers sit at the bar; the team prepares the food as you are watching. The look of the dishes is as stunning as the food itself.

28 BAR JAI-CA
Carrer de Ginebra 13
Barceloneta ④
+34 (0)93 268 32 65
www.barjaica.com

This is a Barceloneta classic, which accounts for the over-full decor. Actually, there are two Jai-ca's: the tiny corner bar with the beer barrels only sells drinks, the tapas bar (just a few steps away, past the pharmacy) is where you'll find fried dough balls with cod, shrimp croquettes and more high calorie, high pleasure tapas.

29 LOS CARACOLES

C/ dels Escudellers 14
El Gòtic ②
+34 (0)93 301 20 41
www.loscaracoles.es

Los Caracoles, also known as Casa Bofarull (after the family who owns it), is the product of two centuries of experience. The interior is a maze-like series of wood panelled rooms, mostly small, some overlooking the kitchen (with authentic coal stove), all of them plastered with pictures of the famous people who've eaten here. It has tons of personality and is well-known for two products: chicken and snails. They also serve other seafood dishes, as well as paellas.

30 CAN MAÑO

Carrer del Baluard 12
Barceloneta ④
+34 (0)93 319 30 82

Extremely affordable seafood, advertised as 'catch of the day'. No pretence, just a great product, prepared with care (and a generous serving of garlic). Can Maño is emblematic of Catalonia's food culture – you don't judge such a culture by the upmarket, expensive places, but by the constant quality of places like this.

27 DOS PALILLOS

5
PAELLA SPECIALISTS

---

31 **CHERIFF**
Carrer de Ginebra 15
Barceloneta ④
+34 (0)93 319 69 84

Word to the wise: paella is rather a Valencian than a Catalonian speciality. There's a lot of bad paella to be found in this city, especially on the Ramblas. Ask any local where to eat paella and the answer will be Cheriff. Do order some extra seafood for starters, do enjoy the kitschy sea view painting, but don't order dessert (it's not at the same level as the paella).

32 **L'ARROSSERIA XÀTIVA**
Carrer del Torrent d'en Vidalet 26
Gràcia ⑪
+34 (0)93 284 85 02
www.grupxativa.com/ arrosseria

The light here hurts the eye, but this small restaurant is a great place to take the entire family. Hearty meals and a pleasant, approachable staff.

33 LA BARRACA

Passeig Marítim 1
Barceloneta ④
+34 (0)93 224 12 53
www.tribuwoki.com/
restaurante/barraca-
barceloneta

What could be more enjoyable than eating fresh fish while overlooking the ocean? La Barraca has great paella, and you could also try the *arroz negro*, a Catalan classic. The waterfront location makes the prices go up: lunch here costs 20 euro (as opposed to 10 or 11 in most Barcelona restaurants), but La Barraca is sophisticated enough to warrant that price.

34 GABRIEL

Avinguda
Diagonal 177
Poblenou ⑤
+34 (0)93 557 98 98

Michelin-star-winning chef Angel Pascual is not one to be pigeon-holed: Gabriel serves a wide variety of food, with rice dishes making a regular appearance. Between 2 and 3 pm, this place will be chock-full of office workers having lunch (good fun for crowd watchers!); in the evening you'll have a better opportunity to savour the food.

35 ELCHE

C/ de Vila i Vilà 71
Poble Sec/Montjuïc ⑥
+34 (0)93 441 30 89
www.elcherestaurant.es

Though rather boring-looking, this restaurant serves several great rice dishes. It boasts having been the first Barcelona restaurant to specialise in real Valencian paella and indeed, you can tell they know what they're doing here. Whether with lobster or chicken, the rice is amazing.

The 5 best

TAPAS BARS

in town

---

36 BAR CAÑETE
Carrer de la Unió 17
Raval ①
+34 (0)93 270 34 58
www.barcanete.com

Bar Cañete offers you a choice: sit by the bar (the blue zone) and eat tapas at high speed, or have a table (in the red zone) and take your time for a leisurely meal. I would recommend the red zone: the beef tartar with wasabi, artichoke tortilla and various other tapas are worth your time. This is really an enjoyable space, modern but without losing the atmosphere of Raval neighbourhood.

37 QUIMET & QUIMET
Carrer del Poeta
Cabanyes 25
Poble Sec/Montjuïc ⑥
+34 (0)93 442 31 42

Quimet & Quimet is a 25-square-metre bodega (don't expect to land one of the two tables) that serves excellent *montaditos*: tapas in a tower-shape. It looks like any other bodega in Barcelona, but don't be fooled: here the food is much better.

38 CAÑOTA
Carrer de Lleida 7
Poble Sec/Montjuïc ⑥
+34 (0)93 325 91 71
www.casadetapas.com

Cañota promises to take its customers to 'Nirtapa'. Their 34-page menu is just as playful as that pun. The tapas are organised by their country or region of origin. This is a good place to try the *navajitas* (razor fish), or Cañota's variation of the classic *ensaladilla rusa* (Russian salad).

39 EL XAMPANYET
C/ de Montcada 22
Born ③
+34 (0)93 319 70 03

The *xampanyet* is a soft, sweet sparkling wine the house recommends to accompany its tapas: olives, sausages, anchovis and the like. Almost a century old, El Xampanyet is a cute and reliable place.

40 GATA MALA
Carrer de Rabassa 37
Gràcia ⑪
+34 636 39 36 10

An always crowded bar, shouting Spanish ladies behind the counter, a regularly changing menu of tapas written on the wall: what's not to like about this 'Bad Pussy'? Besides, the Gràcia district, with its Paris feel, is undervalued by visitors. Gata Mala is just one of the reasons to take the metro up there.

40 GATA MALA

5 places to go for
ASIAN AND INDIAN FOOD

---

41 **SOMODÓ**
C/ Ros de Olano 11
Gràcia ⑪
+34 (0)93 415 65 48
www.sodomo.es

Somodó combines Japanese and Mediterranean cuisine, resulting in delicate, subtle dishes such as scallops tartar, essence of Pad Thai, tuna belly with foie gras... A feast for the senses. There are just two options to choose from: the tasting menu (about 50 euro) and the light version of that.

42 **TOYO**
Carrer del Torrent
de l'Olla 10
Gràcia ⑪
+34 (0)93 459 26 30
*www.restaurante
toyo.com*

Japanese cuisine with a Catalan touch. You can either choose a table or sit by the conveyor belt, picking small dishes as they move past you. The staff just might be the most efficient in town.

43 SURYA MUNTANER

Carrer del Consell
de Cent 236
Eixample ⑨
+34 (0)93 667 87 60
www.surya
barcelona.com

Surya proved itself a great Indian restaurant at Carrer de Pau Claris 92. In 2015 they opened a second venue. Surya Muntaner is a cooler space, with a DJ on Saturday evenings. The food hasn't changed: butter chicken, gambas madras, vegetable *biryani*... All Indian classics, combined with some street food like *pakoras*, *bhel puri* and *somasos*.

44 KOY SHUNKA

Carrer d'en Copons 7
El Gòtic ②
+34 (0)93 412 79 39
www.koyshunka.com

Very sophisticated Japanese cuisine. Forget sushi and explore the tasting menu, with its turbot and Japanese mushrooms, its poached baby squid with *Ume* sauce (pickled Japanese plums sauce) and many other surprises.

45 HIMALAYA

Carrer de Casp 150
Dret de l'Eixample ⑩
+34 (0)93 180 56 14
www.himalaya
restaurant.es

Proper Hindu cuisine avoids beef and is light on meat in general. Himalaya does it really well and gladly explains the dishes on the menu to new customers. The interior could use an upgrade, but don't let that hold you back.

5 places to find
LATIN-AMERICAN DELICACIES

---

46 HOJA SANTA
Avinguda de
Mistral 54
Poble Sec/Montjuïc ⑥
+34 (0)93 348 21 92
www.hojasanta.es

Mexican cuisine is not known for its subtlety. Hoja Santa is a reminder things can be different. The menu (a blend of classic and daring) was created by Mexican chef Paco Méndez and Catalan superstar Albert Adrià. The place is also specialized in *mezcal*, an upmarket version of tequila that will blow your mind with its variety and intensity.

47 BOTECO FOGO / ALQUIMIA FOGO
C/ de Còrsega 231
Eixample ⑨
+34 (0)93 269 28 30
www.alquimiafogo.com

This double restaurant is the brainchild of Brazilian soccer player Dani Alves and chef Joao Alcântara. Downstairs, it's affordable, offering updated Brazilian classics such as *moqueca* (fish stew) and *picandinho* (minced pork). The restaurant upstairs is more expensive and only open for dinner. Here there's only the tasting menu to choose, but not to worry, it will leave you quite speechless.

48 ACHÉ PA TI

Carrer de los
Castillejos 208
Dret de l'Eixample ⑩
+34 (0)93 245 08 65

This budget-friendly Cuban restaurant offers great Caribbean cuisine. Try any rice dish or the *ropa vieja* ('old clothes'): shredded and spiced beef. Since Cuba is the home of the mojito and they make a mean one here, there's no better drink to accompany the food.

49 PUERTO PLATA

Carrer del Tragí 1
Born ③
+34 (0)93 268 36 74

Dominican food means goat. The goat stew with rice and bean is just one example. Barcelona has a large Dominican community and you'll find them here, which is a good sign. The restaurant won't win any design awards, but the noisy, friendly vibe of the place makes you forget about that.

50 AREPAMUNDI

Carrer de N'Aglà 6
El Gòtic ②
+34 (0)93 250 25 06

An *arepa* is a flatbread made of ground maize dough or cooked flour, prominent in the cuisine of Venezuela and Colombia. It comes with various toppings, making this a savoury and not even that unhealthy form of fast food.

50 AREPAMUNDI

5

CHEAP EATS

with great food

---

51 EL BIERZO A TOPE
C/ de la Diputació 159
Eixample ⑨
+34 (0)93 453 70 45
www.elbierzoatope.es

Castillian-Leonese cuisine is known for its cooked *guisos* (dishes) and grilled *asados* (meat). You'll find both of these and more in this lively bar. Good value for little money.

52 CAN PAIXANO: LA CHAMPANERIA
Carrer de la Reina
Cristina 7
Born ③
+34 (0)93 310 08 39
www.canpaixano.com

Paradoxically this tapas bar, with a name including the word 'champagne', is really budget-friendly. That explains why it's usually filled to the brim with people enjoying *jamon iberico* (Spanish ham), *queso semicurado* (a mild Catalan cheese), *pan con tomate* and of course a glass of cava. They also sell hams and cavas, in the back.

53 LAS FERNÁNDEZ
C/ de les Carretes 11
Raval ①
+34 (0)93 443 20 43
www.lasfernandez.com

Food from the León region, namely gammon, venison and sausages. Yes, this is a place to eat meat, which may explain why the entire restaurant is bathed in red. Las Fernández toys with kitsch and gets away with it, safe and sound. A space and a kitchen with personality.

54 PICNIC

Carrer del Comerç 1
Born ③
+34 (0)93 511 66 61
www.picnic-restaurant.com

Picnic hasn't been around that long, but it's already very popular, mostly with the expatriates living in the area. Its kitchen winks at the American South, with its fried green tomatoes and crab cakes.

It feels loungy, with high tables and soft music. Larger groups will feel at ease in the basement space, where a large table is waiting for an entire family to gather around.

55 BAR RAMÓN

Carrer del Comte
Borrell 81
Eixample ⑨
+34 (0)93 325 02 83
www.barramon.com

This is what the Spanish call *un bar de toda la vida* (literally 'a bar of all life'), a run-of-the-mill place. Bar Ramón is certainly that, although they did spruce things up a bit with rock music imagery. The tapas are Catalan classics. Don't just swing by here: make a reservation and show up a bit earlier than promised.

5

places for
MEAT LOVERS

---

56 BARDENI-CALDENI
C/ de València 454
Dret de l'Eixample ⑩
+34 (0)93 232 58 11
www.caldeni.com

Yes, red meat is bad for you. All the more reason, if you're going to eat it anyway, to choose meat of the highest quality. Caldeni is the place for that. Not just because of the quality of the meat, but also because of the chef who cooks it: Dani Lechuga was named 'Young chef 2010' and 'Chef of the year 2011'. Very popular, and a bit pricier than the other restaurants on this list.

57 SUCULENT
Rambla del Raval 43
Raval ①
+34 (0)93 443 65 79
www.suculent.com

Hard to find, classic dishes, with a modern twist. We suggest beef oxtail and trumpet mushroom croquettes for a starter, and calf tail stew with baby carrots and chocolate sauce to continue. Or black pudding with grilled octopus and chickpeas. Ask the waiter which beer goes best with your dish.

58 PORK
C/ del Consolat de
Mar 15
Born ③
+34 (0)93 295 66 36
www.porkboigpertu.com

Pork and nothing but. Would you like an entire suckling pig, or some advice about which portion of the pig's body will suit you best (gastronomically speaking)? Pork provides. When it comes to side-dishes, the potato gratin is a must.

59 NEGRO CARBÓN

Pla de Palau 16
Barceloneta ④
+34 (0)93 319 11 23
*www.negrocarbongrill.
com*

'Black coal' is an Argentinean restaurant, of course specializing in roasted meat and one of the very few places in Barcelona that uses a real Argentinean *parrilla* (grill). Also serves good hamburgers but really, you can find hamburgers anywhere in this city, so go for the real deal here.

60 IGNICIÓ

C/ de Còrsega 244
Eixample ⑨
+34 (0)93 269 34 77
*www.restaurant-
ignicio.com*

Cuina de fum, 'smoke cooking', it says on the windows. At Ignició smoke is considered a spice that can be added to both meat and seafood. Very nice place, with a distinctive concept.

57 SUCULENT

5 welcome solutions for
COELIACS

---

61 COPASETIC

C/ de la Diputació 55
Eixample ⑨
+34 (0)93 532 76 66
*www.copasetic
barcelona.com*

Copasetic asks its customers to inform the waiter about their allergies or intolerances. It helps to reach a 'completely satisfactory' dining experience, which is what *copasetic* means after all. They serve cocktails and 'comfort food': English breakfast, crepes, hamburgers, (pan)cakes, etcetera. The interior is a bit clinical but the food makes up for that.

62 CONESA

C/ de la Llibreteria 1
El Gòtic ②
+34 (0)93 310 13 94
*www.conesaentrepans.
com*

You may think a sandwich shop is unlikely to make it onto a list of coeliac-friendly places, but the hugely popular (expect a queue!) Conesa also has gluten-free options. The sauces used on those (warm and cold) sandwiches are guaranteed gluten-free. There are about 20 options, including vegetarian ones.

63 MAMMAMIA

Carrer de Pallars 230
Poblenou ⑤
+34 600 09 92 81
www.mammamia-bcn.com

Italian cuisine is basically 'Gluten Central', so it's nice to see some Italian restaurants are making an effort. Mammamia serves all the classic pasta dishes (pomodoro, carbonara, pesto, etcetera) in gluten-free versions.

64 LOLITA

C/ de Tamarit 104,
local 2-4
Sant Antoni ⑦
+34 (0)93 424 52 31
www.lolitataperia.com

When Catalonia's star chef Albert Adrià left his tapas bar, his partner Joan Martínez renamed it Lolita and made it his. There are excellent tapas to be found here and a lot of them are gluten-free. Anyone who has read *Lolita* will find the name of this place (and its symbol, an image of flaming red lips) a bit inappropriate, but you can't argue with the quality of the food.

65 LA LLUNA

C/ de Santa Anna 20
El Gòtic ②
+34 (0)93 342 44 79
www.lalluna restaurant.com

Tucked away in an alley off tourist-heavy Carrer de Santa Anna, La Lluna is definitely an old-fashioned kind of place, from the stiff waiters to the quaint decor. Nonetheless, here you'll find a gluten-free dinner you won't forget. The food: duck, entrecote, codfish, gilthead, couscous salad... With gluten-free bread on the tables, of course. Varied and creative, to satisfy the gourmand coeliac sufferer.

5 restaurants that
VEGETARIANS
will love

---

66 LES TRES A LA CUINA
C/ de Sant Lluís 35
Gràcia ⑪
+34 (0)93 105 49 47

The space could do with a bit of sprucing up but Les tres a la cuina is great for lunch. Although they'll occasionally serve meat, there's always a vegetarian option and they're very creative with soups and salads. Three-course lunch for 10 euros.

67 SOPA
C/ de Roc Boronat 114
Poblenou ⑤
+34 (0)93 309 56 76
www.sopabarcelona.
com

Sopa is a big and bright vegetarian and vegan restaurant with macrobiotic influences. Given its name, it's not a big surprise soup is an important feature on their menu. All soups (e.g. carrot and orange soup, or pumpkin and sweet potato soup) are vegan. A 10 euro lunch menu includes a soup, a salad and a second dish, for example a stew of mijo, vegetables and lentils.

68 LA VITAMÍNICA DE HORTA
Passeig de
Maragall 413
Horta-Guinardó
+34 (0)93 357 30 71

A typical neighbourhood restaurant gone vegetarian. It's very relaxed and homely and the lunch menu is worth a detour. They show the different plates in the window, which is convenient for visitors who don't speak Spanish.

69 CAT BAR

Carrer de la Bòria 17
Born ③
+34 693 584 700

The mirrors on the wall turn out to be cat's eyes. There are drawings of people with animal heads on the walls. Cat Bar is a good example of how you can turn a tiny space into something distinctive. This vegan restaurant is strict about its food choices but does have a weakness for beer: Catalan craft beers, to be exact. A place with a character.

70 PAPPA SVEN

C/ de Villarroel 22
Sant Antoni ⑦
+34 (0)93 292 82 39
www.pappasven.es

At first you'll notice the interior (a cross between an old Ikea catalogue and the inside of a dollhouse), but you'll soon get distracted by the food. This Swedish restaurant is great at herring dishes and salmon. They sell Swedish beer and some other national delicacies. And the thing that will knock you out cold is not the bill but their liquor shots.

67 SOPA

5 places to go for a
LOVELY BRUNCH

---

71 BRUNCH & CAKE
C/ Enric Granados 19
Eixample ⑨
+34 (0)93 200 28 72
www.cupcakes
barcelona.com/
shops-brunchcake

Brunch here is such a pleasure, that it's worth queuing in the street on Saturday and Sunday mornings. Try several variations on eggs Benedict, turkey bagels or a pulled chicken cronut. Too heavy? Try the 'super food salads'. Also the cakes are tempting. There are three branches of Brunch & Cake in Eixample now, but the original one on Carrer Enric Granados remains the best.

72 MARMALADA
C/ de la Riera Alta 4
Raval ①
+34 (0)93 442 39 66
www.marmalade
barcelona.com

Interior-wise, Marmalada certainly is a strange place. The middle part of the restaurant looks like it's trying to be hip, but the corridors on the side look classy and old-fashioned, with lots of dark wood panelling. It's grand and cosy at the same time. This is *the* place to overcome a hangover, thanks to the amazing brunch options and a selection of great cocktails. A guilty pleasure, really.

73 DOSTRECE

C/ del Carme 40
Raval ①
+34 (0)93 301 73 06
www.dostrece.net

The windows of DosTrece are note-worthy for two reasons. One: Barcelona restaurants tend to be oriented inwards, while here you're invited to people-watch as you are enjoying the hearty, American-style food. Two: there's a painted skull on one of the windows, making the restaurant easy to spot. It's maybe the most 'New York' of restaurants, right up its emphasis on vegan food.

74 TIMELINE BAR

C/ de la Providència 3
Gràcia ⑪
+34 (0)93 217 79 38

A tiny but classy place: it looks like a cross between a flea market and a boudoir. The brunch is presented as a buffet and runs the gamut from healthy (smoked salmon) over sweet (those cakes!) to boozy (all-you-can-drink Bloody Marys).

75 VERMUT MIDDAY SESSIONS

Carrer de Bergara 8
Raval ①
+34 (0)93 481 67 67
www.hotelpulitzer.es

Need an excuse to enter a luxury hotel? The Pulitzer Hotel opens its terrace to the public on various occasions. The Vermut Sessions, for instance, take place on Saturdays and Sundays, between midday and 4 pm. Is vermut not your taste? The Pulitzer terrace happens to be known for its gin tonics as well. Almost forgot: they make gourmet sandwiches and tapas.

5 places to go for a
GOOD AND
INEXPENSIVE LUNCH

76 **P'TIT BISTRO**
C/ de la Diputació 294
Dret de l'Eixample ⑩
+34 (0)93 412 52 43

Anywhere in Barcelona you can have lunch for about 11 euros, but obviously it's not always a memorable experience. P'tit Bistro mixes French and Catalan cuisine with terrific results. Try the *arroz negro* or one of the rabbit dishes. The lemon meringue pie is to die for.

77 **CENT FOCS**
Carrer de Balmes 16
Eixample ⑨
+34 (0)93 412 00 95
www.centfocs.com

This spacious restaurant, a stone's throw away from Plaça Catalunya, is a Barcelona institution. The evening's gourmet menu is a bit pricier, but over lunch (10,95 euros) the quality/price balance is hard to beat.

78 **CASA JAIME**
Carrer del Consell
de Cent 222
Eixample ⑨
+34 (0)93 189 32 22
www.casajaime.rest

The interior looks like a vintage furniture store, but a bit rougher. With its Catalan and Spanish classics on the menu, it's the ideal lunch stop for people discovering the Eixample neighbourhood. Very good service.

79 EL CASAL

**Plaça de Víctor
Balaguer 5
Born ③
+34 (0)93 268 40 04
*www.elcasalcafe.com***

This French-owned restaurant, two minutes away from Santa María del Mar church, is deliciously dynamic. Both the sandwich and the lunch options change daily and incorporate culinary influences from around the globe. And all that for a very good price.

80 LA RITA

**Carrer d'Aragó 279
Dret de l'Eixample ⑩
+34 (0)93 487 23 76
*www.grupandilana.
com/es/restaurantes/
la-rita-restaurant***

La Rita is the kind of place that looks way more chic than it really is. And like Cent Focs, you can snatch up a three-course lunch for about 11 euros. Good quality, extremely fast service.

79 **EL CASAL**

The 5 best restaurants
AROUND THE RAMBLAS

81 **BAR LOBO**
Carrer del Pintor
Fortuny 3
Raval ①
+34 (0)93 481 53 46

There's something pleasantly grand about this restaurant with its glass façade. You can sit outside, next to the rack with fresh herbs, or inside, downstairs or upstairs, overlooking the vibrant little square.

82 **EL GRAN CAFÉ**
Carrer d'Avinyó 9
El Gòtic ②
+34 (0)93 318 79 86
www.restaurant
elgrancafe.com

Here, the gleaming wood and old-fashioned veneer fills the customer with confidence that he'll get dependable, old-fashioned Catalan cuisine – which happens to be exactly what El Gran Café has to offer.

83 **LES QUINZE NITS**
Plaça Reial 6
El Gòtic ②
+34 (0)93 317 30 75

Les Quinze Nits is part of a chain and yet it effortlessly combines style with good food for very little money. The fish here is especially praise-worthy, like the seared tuna or the cod with *aioli* (a Catalan mayonnaise with lots of garlic).

84 LA CREMA CANELA

Passatge de Madoz 6
El Gòtic ②
+34 (0)93 318 27 44

La Crema Canela belongs to the same dependable chain as Les Quinze Nits. *Canela* means cinnamon; the chefs here like to use all kinds of spices, as in the salmon *fagotti* with fresh-herb cream or the salads with fresh cheese, bacon and basil vinaigrette. A cosy place, close to Plaça Reial, where all the night clubs are.

85 MARGARITA BLUE

Carrer de Josep
Anselm Clavé 6
El Gòtic ②
+34 (0)93 412 54 89
www.margaritablue.
com

This is a good place for Tex-Mex cooking: fried green tomatoes, fajitas and enchiladas, some even in low-calorie variations. You don't just come here to eat, though: Margarita Blue is named after a cocktail for a reason. It all results in a bustling atmosphere that can be very energizing.

81 BAR LOBO

5 *irresistible*
BAKERIES AND OTHER SWEET PLACES

---

86 HOFFMAN

C/ del Flassaders 44
Born ③
+34 (0)93 268 82 21
*www.hofmann-bcn.com/
pasteleria*

Hoffman is a school (for cooks and pastry chefs), then a restaurant, a tavern and a bakery. They have astonishing croissants with several fillings and some very beautiful cakes. If you're visiting around Easter or Christmas, look out for the elaborate chocolate decorations in the shop window.

87 LA PASTISSERIA

Carrer d'Aragó 228
Eixample ⑨
+34 (0)93 451 84 01
*www.lapastisseria
barcelona.com*

He's still in his twenties, but Josep Maria Rodriguez has already won the title of 'World Pastry Champion'. His creations are simply stunning: high-quality ingredients in surprising new shapes, so beautiful you won't want to break them with your spoon. His shop also sells his book, *Sweetology*.

88 BALUARD

Carrer del Baluard 38
Barceloneta ④
+34 (0)93 221 12 08
*www.baluard
barceloneta.com.com*

Three generations of bakers have worked here and some of the old habits (like using a wood-fired oven) have survived. Baluard is the *éminence grise* of Barcelona bakeries. The fruit tartlets alone are a reason to visit, and we'll bet good money you won't be able to resist the bread either.

89 FORN MISTRAL

**Ronda de Sant
Antoni 96**
Sant Antoni ⑦
+34 (0)93 301 80 37
www.fornmistral.com

The *ensaimada* is a pastry product from Mallorca; in Barcelona it's about as common as a croissant. It's round and snail-shaped and the magic ingredient is saïm. It may interest as well as disgust you to know this is a kind of pork lard. Be that as it may, you have to try an *ensaimada*, and Bakery Mistral is far and beyond the best place in town for that.

90 LA COLMENA

Plaça de l'Angel 12
El Gòtic ②
+34 (0)93 315 13 56
*www.pastisseria
lacolmena.com*

Right next to metro stop Jaume I, La Colmena is lying in wait for its next victim, lured in by the stacks of meringues in the shop window. Like the store itself, the candy here looks homey and traditional. No bread, just teeth-destroying goodness.

86 HOFFMAN

THE BIKE CLUB

70 PLACES TO GO FOR A DRINK AND PARTY

5
COFFEE BARS
baristas love

---

91 **CAFÉS EL MAGNÍFICO**
Carrer de l'Argenteria 64
Born ③
+34 (0)93 319 39 75
www.cafes elmagnifico.com

Freshly ground beans, straightforward advice and (if you can't wait until you get home) a coffee to go, made by a fine barista: El Magnifico is the real deal in coffee expertise. Prefer tea? They sell that too. The large cookies they keep enticingly close to the counter are a must.

92 **SATAN'S COFFEE CORNER**
C/ de l'Arc de Sant Ramon del Call 11
El Gòtic ②
+34 666 22 25 99
www.satanscoffee.com

The espresso machine here has had the plastic case removed, so you can see its insides. It's a wink at the customers: Satan's Coffee Corner is about the content, not about the bow people can put around things. Lunch and breakfast suggestions are carefully rhymed with coffee types. Also sells an interesting collection of magazines.

93 CAELUM

Carrer de la Palla 8
El Gòtic ②
+34 (0)93 302 69 93
www.caelumbarcelona.
com

Caelum Bakery sells pastries and cookies made by monks and nuns in Catalonian monasteries, and the adjoining coffee shop adds caffeine to that (already very convincing) offer. If you haven't reached heaven (*caelum*) by then, you can choose one of various liqueurs. Pick up a jar of artisan jam on the way out.

94 MESÓN DEL CAFÉ

C/ de la Llibreteria 16
El Gòtic ②
+34 (0)93 315 07 54

Whereas most coffee bars strive to be as cool and intense as possible, Mesón del Café goes for yesterday's laid-back approach. The interior basically hasn't been touched since 1909 and the coffee machine is supposed to be the oldest in town. It looks surprisingly like a German beer bar, but if you can get over the culture shock, you'll notice they do make a wicked cup of coffee.

95 NØMAD COFFEE

Passatge Sert 12
Born ③
+34 628 56 62 35
www.nomadcoffee.es

Barista Jordi Mestre has won multiple awards. At Nømad Coffee he roasts the beans himself. The available coffees change regularly, since Mestre and his partner-in-coffee Kim Ossenblok only work with fresh beans and so are dependent on the seasons. Passatge Sert isn't that easy to find, but this beautiful little street is worth looking for. You'll also find restaurant Casa Lolea here and a nice French furniture store, Ici et là.

5
WINE BARS
you'll never want to leave

---

96 BAR BRUTAL

Carrer de la Barra de Ferro 1
Born ③
+34 (0)93 295 47 97
www.cancisa.cat

Bar Brutal is a Barcelona must. It consists of two parts, one of those being Can Cisa, a cave-like wine store, decorated in earth tones (entrance: Carrer de la Princesa 14). Another part is an equally stark but more outlandish looking bar, called Bar Brutal. The store specializes in ecological and biodynamic wines.

97 BAR ZIM

C/ de la Dagueria 20
El Gòtic ②
+34 (0)93 412 65 48
www.barzimbcn.com

At this tiny cupboard-like bar you can enjoy a good glass of wine (served with knowledge but without any form of posh behaviour) and maybe a *peton* (Catalan for 'kiss'): a small cheese and marmalade tapa. The bar has a terrace around the corner, on Plaça de Sant Just.

98 MONVÍNIC

C/ de la Diputació 249
Eixample ⑨
+34 (0)93 272 61 87
www.monvinic.com

Monvínic aspires to be more than a wine bar and a restaurant: it's a centre for wine culture. It has its own (modest) library and a giant bodega with international wines. Author and wine-lover Jay McInnery came, saw and loved it: "I haven't been to every wine bar in the world but Monvínic in Barcelona is certainly the best I've been to in recent memory." (*The Wall Street Journal*)

99 ZONA D'OMBRA

Carrer de Sant
Domènec del Coll 12
El Gòtic ②
+34 (0)93 500 58 02
www.zonadombra.es

Zona d'Ombra was inspired by Italian wine bars, so the wine list is heavy on Italian wines. No one will complain: they've got excellent taste here. As a bonus, they have a terrace on a tiny square, tucked away in a Gothic labyrinth.

100 LA VINYA DEL SENYOR

Plaça de Santa
Maria 5
Born ③
+34 (0)93 310 33 79

Major tourist attractions tend to attract cheap bars and doubtful restaurants, and yet, right in front of the Santa Maria del Mar is this highly reliable wine bar. Don't feel bad if the terrace is full (it tends to be); the inside is just as nice. Incidentally, if you leave the bar and turn left, you're in Carrer de l'Anisadeta, the shortest street in Barcelona.

5 nice bars for a
DRINK WITH THE LOCALS

---

101 BAR PIETRO

**Travessera de
Gràcia 197**
Gràcia ⑪
+34 697 27 08 22

Every Barcelona neighbourhood has its own market; the best known of those is of course Boqueria (on the Ramblas). Bar Pietro is right next to the Mercat de l'Abaceria, one of the Gràcia markets. It's where the locals go for a quick drink or coffee after shopping. The beer is cheap and the Germinal sandwich (ham, brie, tomato marmalade) a treat.

102 MADAME JASMINE

Rambla del Raval 22
Raval ①
+34 630 10 86 80

It doesn't get much more quaint than Madame Jasmine. The burgundy light, the kitschy decoration, the old-fashioned porn pictures behind the bar, the rather disturbing photos in the toilet... Madame Jasmine is a cross between David Lynch and Pedro Almodóvar. And yet it's also a very cosy place where they serve a wily mojito.

103 LA PRINCIPAL

C/ de Sepúlveda 186
Sant Antoni ⑦
+34 (0)93 325 30 89

They make a fine salad here, but the atmosphere is the main reason to visit La Principal. Whether it's for the first drink (before launching yourself into the Eixample or Raval nightlife) or to while away a Sunday afternoon on the terrace, La Principal is the place to be. At all cost avoid using the upstairs toilet.

104 ABSENTA 1893

Carrer de l'Hospital 75
Raval ①
+34 (0)93 270 35 64

Can you drink absinthe here? Yes, but it's not the local specialty so don't bother. What's more important is that this is your place if you want to get away from the tourist bars and have a drink for next to nothing, surrounded by locals who just left the office. There are other bars called 'Absenta' in the neighbourhood, so look out for the '1893'.

105 GUIXOT

Carrer de la Riereta 8
Raval ①
+34 (0)93 329 95 53
www.guixot.cat

Guixot specializes in really tasty sandwiches and crêpes. The interior is sparse to the extreme, but at least this isn't one of the many places in town where the interior is better than the food. Here they serve (among other things) the excellent September sandwich: eggplant, zucchini, onion, brie cheese and chicken.

5 tasty
COCKTAILS AND
SPECIALTIES BARS

106 PARADISO

C/ de Rera Palau 4
Born ③
+34 (0)93 360 72 22
www.paradiso.cat

In December 2016 Paradiso was crowned the city's best cocktail bar, and rightly so. From the grandiose yet cosy interior design, over the exquisite cocktails and their creative presentation, to the pastrami sandwiches on the menu, everything at Paradiso is close to perfect. Personal favourite: a whisky cocktail called 'Great Gatsby'.

107 BALIUS BAR

C/ de Pujades 196
Poblenou ⑤
+34 (0)93 315 86 50
www.baliusbar.com

Cocktail bars can be haughty places, almost too posh to be enjoyable. Balius Bar is the exact opposite: a neighbourhood bar in Barcelona's Berlin-like Poblenou neighbourhood. The double façade of this corner bar demands to be photographed.

108 BETTY FORD'S

Carrer de Joaquín
Costa 56
Raval ①
+34 (0)93 304 13 68
www.bettyfords.es

This ironically named cocktail bar serves excellent drinks, succulent hamburgers and shows strange old movies while you try to make yourself heard over the noise of the crowd. Carrer de Joaquín Costa used to be a bit seedy, but its recent evolution is interesting: take a walk up and down the street and you'll find cocktail bars and halal butchers, hipster spots and laundrettes.

109 SPEAKEASY / DRY MARTINI

Carrer d'Aribau 162
Eixample ⑨
+34 (0)93 217 50 80
www.drymartiniorg.
com/locales/speakeasy/

You enter cocktail bar Dry Martini by walking through the front door; to reach the restaurant Speakeasy you have to go through the kitchen! In 2015 Dry Martini was the only Spanish bar on 'The world's 50 best bars' list. The jury said: "Everything (...) has been carefully considered, from the things you see – such as the slick, white coated team tending bar (...) and the carefully curated cocktail art collection – to the way you're made to feel, courtesy of the well-chosen soundtrack and exemplary service."

110 OLD FASHIONED

C/ de Santa Teresa 1
Gràcia ⑪
+34 (0)93 368 52 77
www.oldfashioned
cocktailbar.com

Ironically the Old Fashioned that is served in this bar is not that old-fashioned. Here Don Draper's drink (usually whisky, sugar and citrus rind) comes with roasted nuts, and has been renamed Fashionista. And it's far from the only excellent 'author cocktail' on the menu.

The 5 best bars
ALONG THE BEACH

---

111 EL PACÍFICO
C/ de la Vila Joiosa 52
Barceloneta ④
+34 (0)93 225 71 64
www.elpacifico.es

The closer to the water, the more expensive bars and restaurants tend to get, and unfortunately, they aren't always worth it. A general rule to follow in Barcelona: stay closer to the Barceloneta streets than to the waterfront. Try El Pacífico for instance: it has a beach view, a stark, pleasant interior, and good wine and cocktails.

112 MAMAROSA BEACH
Passeig del Mare
Nostrum 19-21
Barceloneta ④
+34 (0)93 312 35 86
www.mamarosabeach.com

You won't find anything classier than this bar on the ground floor of the W Hotel. The W Hotel basically seals off one side of the beach so the view goes all the way to Frank Gehry's *Peix*. Mamarosa Beach serves pastas, pizzas and other Italian classics, but it's better just to lounge here.

113 SANTA MARTA
C/ de Grau i Torras 59
Barceloneta ④
+34 691 23 68 02

A chunk of Italy in Barcelona, this colourful bar serves the cuisine of its owner's country (pizza, *piadina*) and mixes a good cocktail – both of spirits and of atmosphere. After all, with the pleasantly kitschy interior and the pop music they play, it's amazing that having an aperitif here can be so relaxing.

114 AROLA

Carrer de la Marina 19
Poblenou ⑤
+34 (0)93 221 10 00
www.hotelarts
barcelona.com/en/
Dining/Arola

The Arola at Hotel Arts may be best known as a restaurant, but few people know that it's also home to one of Barcelona's most luxurious cocktail bars. Enjoy the mouth-watering creations of master mixologist Diego in the chic bar or outdoors on the stylish terrace with a view across the Mediterranean, while local DJs spin their tunes.

115 VASO DE ORO

Carrer de Balboa 6
Barceloneta ④
+34 (0)93 319 30 98
www.vasodeoro.com

Five minutes away from the beach, you'll find this pleasant little bar, renowned for its beers. They also serve no-nonsense classic tapas. It's brown and lively and will make you want to stay a bit longer.

113   SANTA MARTA

The 5 hippest
HIPSTER BARS

---

116 THE BIKE CLUB
Carrer de Sepúlveda 6
Sant Antoni ⑦
+34 (0)93 179 13 71
www.thebikeclub.es

You can have some quick repair work done on your bike here, while enjoying a coffee or a freshly squeezed juice. Even better, you can also rent bikes, and when you're tired from exploring the city by bike, The Bike Club's Korean-style tacos and Mexican burritos will pick you up in just a couple of minutes.

117 COSMO
C/ Enric Granados 3
Eixample ⑨
+34 (0)93 105 79 92
www.galeriacosmo.com

In the back this is an art gallery for young artists, in the front it's a place to enjoy a salad, a freshly-squeezed juice (there are eight varieties) or a slice of cake. Expect lots of young people working on their Macbook or checking their iPhone.

118 MITTE
Carrer de Bailèn 86
Dret de l'Eixample ⑩
+34 647 44 49 16
www.mitte-barcelona.com

Another art gallery and bar, but compared to Cosmo (the previous address in this list), Mitte has a nicer space, aiming for grandeur. You can have breakfast and lunch here, but no dinner, and Wi-Fi is free.

119 **BAR CALDERS**

C/ del Parlament 25
Sant Antoni ⑦
+34 (0)93 329 93 49

Bar Calders is a small space with high ceilings, looking Catalan on the inside and looking more like southern Spain on its colourful patio. Order the homemade hummus and have a *vermut*; you may also be tempted to stick around for pizza. Calders was a Catalan poet, by the way.

120 **MARTI CREATIVE CAFÉ**

Carrer de Roger
de Lluria 51
Dret de l'Eixample ⑩
+34 (0)93 488 35 48

Not every day is a holiday. If you're in town for a meeting but you don't want to take your clients or co-workers to a formal, fancy place, then this alternative bakery slash coffee shop slash snackbar is a good idea. It looks stylish on the outside, cosy on the inside and the smell will make it impossible not to enjoy some baked goods.

116 **THE BIKE CLUB**

5 happy
GAY BARS

---

121 EL CANGREJO
C/ de Villarroel 88
Eixample ⑨

Loud interior, red light, Spanish pop music and the occasional drag performance: Cangrejo (Lobster) is the kind of gay bar you see in the movies and yes, it's just as much fun as it looks like in those movies. Attracts a young crowd.

122 MUSEUM
C/ de Sepúlveda 178
Sant Antoni ⑦
+34 (0)93 325 18 31

Two bars, a lot of fake art and plenty of television screens showing the music videos to the songs you hear. Museum is popular with men who frequent gyms but also with groups of friends who just want to have a good time dancing. On weekend nights it gets filled to the brim between 1 and 3 am.

123 SKYBAR, AXEL HOTEL
Carrer Aribau 33
Eixample ⑨
+34 (0)93 323 93 93
*www.axelhotels.com/
hoteles/barcelona*

Axel Hotel is the number one gay hotel in Barcelona. Of course it needed a fancy cocktail bar on the roof. So there you have it: a bit more formal than most gay bars but very relaxed. Comes with a nice view over Eixample.

124 ZELIG

Carrer del Carme 116
Raval ①
+34 (0)93 125 01 35
www.zelig-barcelona.
com

The friendliest of the city's gay bars. The staff are a joy to watch, and apart from the regular drinks they have some personal cocktails as well (such as the wodka-based 'Swedish Bitch'). During the day food is served, mostly Italian. There's a terrace on the square across the street.

125 VERSAILLES

Passatge Valeri
Serra 3
Eixample ⑨
+34 (0)93 454 61 72

Decorated like the inside of an insane jewellery box, this bar certainly hasn't stolen its name. A good, quiet place for a drink and a chat.

5 original
CONCEPT BARS

---

126 CASSETTE BAR
Carrer de l'Est 11
Raval ①
+34 (0)93 302 85 09

Lamps made of old tapes, an Etch-a-Sketch and lots of plastic stuff that once upon a time (namely in the 80s) made sense to people. Cassette Bar is one of the most striking-looking places in Barcelona. The music is the more alternative side of the 80s and 90s.

127 FÀBRICA MORITZ
Ronda de Sant Antoni 39-41
Sant Antoni ⑦
+34 (0)93 426 00 50
www.moritz.com/es/seccion/fbrica-moritz-barcelona

What was once the old brewery of Catalan beer brand Moritz is now a bar slash restaurant slash *brasserie* slash bakery slash bookshop. The founders are aiming for extreme coolness and it's working. With its many doors and compartments Fàbrica Moritz feels like a world onto itself. The building, incidentally, was renovated by famous architect Jean Nouvel: take a good look around, there's more to see than you think.

128 **BHARMA**

Carrer de Pere IV 93
Poblenou ⑤
+34 (0)93 667 09 13

Remember the time when we thought the plot of *Lost* would make sense in the end? That time is revived in Bharma, the *Lost* bar. Good food at lunchtime, a loungy atmosphere in the evening. For the fans, everything's here: the crashed Oceanic plane, the strange sequence of numbers, the caves, the Dharma Initiative symbols...

129 **EL NACIONAL**

Passeig de Gràcia
24bis
Eixample ⑨
+34 (0)93 518 50 53
www.elnacionalbcn.com

El Nacional is not one bar, it's several bars and several restaurants, sharing one space which until recently was nothing but an abandoned car park. El Nacional is very fancy and quite expensive, but you simply have to go, if just to admire the various decorating styles of the bars. Pick up a copy of El Nacional's own little gazette to learn everything about this place.

130 **AVESTA**

Carrer de Marquet 2
El Gòtic ②
+34 (0)93 310 73
www.avesta.es

Butterflies and banknotes, symbols and souvenirs... Avesta deals in weirdness. The chairs made out of logs should tip us off: this is the David Lynch universe, the kind of bar Lynch would have his characters meet. Only there's no languorous symphonic music here: Avesta plays Spanish pop and rock from the 80s. As a whole it shouldn't work, but it does.

The 5
OLDEST BARS
in town

---

131 ELS 4GATS

Carrer de Montsió 3
El Gòtic ②
+34 (0)93 302 41 40
www.4gats.com

Fashioned after the French cabaret Le chat noir, Els 4gats was meant to feed the body as well as the soul. It quickly became the hangout for Barcelona's artists and intellectuals; at one point it even had its own cultural magazine. The interior mixes elements of a traditional Catalan tavern with artistic touches. The lamps and furniture give the whole a slightly medieval feel.

132 LONDON BAR

Carrer Nou de la Rambla 34
Raval ①
+34 (0)93 318 52 61

London Bar used to be the hangout for the likes of Dalí, Picasso and Hemingway. The interior hasn't changed in over a century. You could call this 'faded art-deco splendour' and it's very easy to love. They have lots of little concerts in the bar, so if you like it in the morning – there's something very classy about having your first cup of coffee here – do go back in the evening.

133 CAFÉ DE L'OPERA

Les Rambles 74
Raval ①
+34 (0)93 317 75 85
www.cafeoperabcn.com

Café de l'Opera started out as a *chocolateria* (chocolate café) sometime before 1831, then became a restaurant and found its current shape in 1929. It looks a little like a stage inside, as if you're waiting for a larger-than-life character to enter. The mirrors are engraved with feminine figures. A pleasantly old-fashioned place for a drink.

134 LA CONFITERÍA

C/ de Sant Pau 128
Poble Sec/Montjuïc ⑥
+34 (0)93 140 54 35
www.myspace.com/
laconfiteria

Why is a bar called 'the confectionery store'? Because it used to be just that. Its modernist decorations were preserved, as well as the glass cupboards and the shop windows. It's a slightly Parisian-feeling bit of history and worth a visit.

135 CAN CULLERETES

C/ d'en Quintana 5
El Gòtic ②
+34 (0)93 317 30 22
www.culleretes.com

According to the Guinness book of records Can Culleretes (founded in 1786) is the second-oldest bar/restaurant in Spain. They call the various spaces 'salons' and they have murals of 19-century Spaniards enjoying themselves.

132 LONDON BAR

5 great bars to just
SIT BACK AND RELAX

___

136 BITTE
Carrer de Londres 87
Eixample ⑨
+34 (0)93 667 08 40
www.bittebcn.blogspot.
com

So where do you go when Barcelona has filled you with so many new impressions you need to sit down and process? Bitte is a wonderful option. It has its own botanical garden, is handsomely decorated and serves surprising, cosmopolitan lunches. It's where students go to focus on their work.

137 PATCHWORK CONCEPT BAR
Avinguda
del Paral-lel 98
Poble Sec/Montjuïc ⑥
+34 (0)93 250 48 29

Patchwork is a new and welcome addition: a coffee bar with a terrace, yummy bagels (some with home-made pesto) and a nice look. Lots of black here, with lamps you expect sitting on someone's desk hanging from the ceiling.

138 CAFÉ COMETA
Carrer
del Parlament 20
Sant Antoni ⑦
+34 (0)93 007 32 03
www.cafecometa.com

Café Cometa is the juice bar where you'll spend more time than you planned. It's smaller, but the second floor offers perfect seats to relax. You can also have various bowls of cereal.

139 OVAL

C/ de València 199
Eixample ⑨
+34 (0)93 010 26 47
www.ovalbcn.com

The last couple of years, Barcelona has been obsessed with the gourmet hamburger. The trend is winding down now but the best hamburger places are still around. Oval gives you the opportunity to mix and match with a lot of ingredients and nobody will mind if you hang around for an hour or two after your meal. Oval looks like a loft, with some pretty design furniture.

140 LAIE LIBRERÍA-CAFÉ

C/ de Pau Claris 85
Dret de l'Eixample ⑩
+34 (0)93 318 17 39
www.laierestaurants.es/
pau_claris

Bookshop Laie hardly has any books in English, but even non-Spanish speakers can be attracted to the bar and restaurant on the first floor: a pleasant place with natural light and good food, free Wi-Fi, plus a terrace. If you come to lunch early – which in Spain means: between 1 pm and 1:30 pm – coffee is free.

139 OVAL

5 *places you*
CAN'T LEAVE
WITHOUT A BOTTLE

---

141 FREIXENET CELLARS
Carrer de Joan Sala 2
Sant Sadurní d'Anoia
+34 (0)93 891 70 00
RESERVATIONS:
+34 (0)93 891 70 96
www.freixenet.es

Catalonia's best-known drink abroad is cava: just as good as champagne (the Catalans say) and cheaper. You can get it everywhere in town but if you've got the time, take a trip to the Freixenet cellars (30 minutes outside of Barcelona). The tours come in Spanish and English.

142 GIN CORNER
Carrer de Rocafort 19
Sant Antoni ⑦
+34 (0)93 423 43 14

Feeling ready to stop buying your gin at the supermarket? At Gin Corner you can learn about gin (during one of their gin tasting evenings), sip it right there or buy a bottle in their physical or online store. They have a marvellous taste and they'll help you develop one too.

143 EL BOMBÍN BAR BODEGA
Carrer de Bilbao 85
Poblenou ⑤
+34 (0)93 269 23 89

The little green terrace in front may look hipster, but on the inside, El Bonbín is pretty much what you expect a bodega to look like: brown and sort of rough. 'Bombín' means bowler hat, which is why the lampshades are bowler hats. Have a drink, do not miss the tapas and leave with at least one bottle.

144 **VILA VINITECA**

Carrer dels Agullers 7
Born ③
+34 (0)93 777 70 17
www.vilaviniteca.es

Vila Viniteca used to be a simple green-grocer's store – hence the bananas hanging next to the door – but these days it's a veritable gourmet trap. On one side of the street is the wine shop, on the other side Vila Viniteca sells cheeses, hams and meat and a selection of delicatessen that will have you salivate (and your creditcard working overtime).

145 **ELS SORTIDORS DEL PARLAMENT**

C/ del Parlament 53
Sant Antoni ⑦
+34 (0)93 441 16 02
www.elssortidors.com

Els Sortidors del Parlament focuses on wines from Catalonia, and some Catalan artisan draft beers as well. It's a large space, with wine barrels as the major design element. It's located on the hip and happening Carrer del Parlament, a street chock-full of great restaurants and bars.

142 GIN CORNER

144 VILA VINITECA

5
POSH BARS
for the rich and famous

---

146 BOCA CHICA
**Passatge de la
Concepció 12
Eixample** ⑨
+34 (0)93 467 51 49
*www.bocagrande.cat/
boca-chica*

If you're hoping to have a drink with a soccer player or another celebrity, than visiting this fancy cocktail bar gives you a good chance. To avoid any confusion: Boca Grande (Big Mouth) is a restaurant, specialized in rice dishes and fish, whereas Boca Chica (Small Mouth) is the adjoining cocktail bar. Prices are steep: you'll need a couple of cocktails to get over the shock.

147 GATSBY
**Carrer de Tuset 19-21
Gràcia** ⑪
+34 (0)93 700 44 53
*www.gatsbybarcelona.
com*

Live performances by singers and dancers in top hats and bathing suits, aiming for a 1920s atmosphere. The food is decent enough, but really this place is all about bling. The entire Barça team has been known to celebrate victories here. Don't forget to dress up.

148 SOHO HOUSE BARCELONA

Plaça del Duc de
Medinaceli 4
El Gòtic ②
+34 (0)93 220 46 00
*www.sohohouse
barcelona.com/en*

This exclusive clubs attracts a young and creative crowd, who come to hang out on one of the several floors and share ideas. You have to be invited or pay a steep entry fee. A restaurant is about to open on the ground floor.

149 ECLIPSE BAR
HOTEL W

Plaça de la Rosa
dels Vents 1
Barceloneta ④
+34 (0)93 295 28 00
*www.eclipse-barcelona.
com*

W Barcelona is the sail-shaped hotel that seals off the Barcelona beach. Even if you're not staying there, you can take the elevator to the top floor, to enjoy the sea view while sipping a cocktail in the Eclipse Bar. Short pants and similar beach wear are not allowed.

150 ROCA MOO
(HOTEL OMM)

C/ del Rosselló 265
Eixample ⑨
+34 (0)93 445 40 00
*www.hotelomm.com/
roca-barcelona/
roca-moo*

You will always remember your visit to Roca Moo restaurant if you taste the dazzling Golden Egg, a brittle caramel shell with creamy potatoes and toasted corn inside. The Golden Egg sums up this place beautifully: it's more about the looks than about the actual product. Roca Moo is where you take someone who needs to be impressed.

5 *clubs to*
DANCE THE NIGHT AWAY

---

151 LA BOÎTE
Les Rambles 33
Raval ①
+34 (0)93 319 17 89

During the weekends, 3 am is a pivotal time in Barcelona: it's when most bars close their doors and if you want to keep on partying, you'll have to move to a dance club. La Boîte signals 3 am by moving from disco to harder house. It's highly enjoyable both before and after 3 am though.

152 ALFA
C/ Gran de Gràcia 36
Gràcia ⑪
+34 (0)93 415 18 24
www.alfabar.cat

No, this place is not cool. The Spanish call this *cutre*, which is something in between kitsch and crap. And yet, after midnight the club gets into a communal trance, everyone shouting along to Spanish and American rock songs. You don't need to be seen here; you just come to enjoy yourself. Effortlessly.

153 JAMBOREE
Plaça Reial 17
El Gòtic ②
+34 (0)93 319 17 89
www.masimas.com/ jamboree

There's jazz at Jamboree, but Jamboree is more. The jazz concerts take place in the early evenings (about 8 pm), and afterwards it's time to party with pop, rock or hip-hop, starting after midnight. Two clubs, one admission fee.

154 HARLEM JAZZ CLUB

**Carrer de Comtessa
de Sobradiel 8**
El Gòtic ②
+34 (0)93 310 07 55
www.harlemjazzclub.es

You don't always need a beat to start dancing. Early jazz, blues and funk can do the trick just as well. Harlem Jazz Club has concerts most days of the week and the friendliest vibe a dance club can have. You can tell people find each other through the music here. Everyone should experience this vibe at least once.

155 MOOG

C/ de l'Arc del Teatre 3
Raval ①
+34 (0)93 319 17 89
*www.masimas.com/
moog*

A long narrow bar, ending in a square dance floor. Moog (originally: Moog Electronic Dancing Club) is the coolest place imaginable to dance yourself into a sweat. It boasts being the starting point of the careers of many DJs. It doesn't matter whether you're a DJ expert or not: this is a place to party hard.

5 *times of*
FUN ON THE STREETS

---

156 FESTA MAJOR DE GRÀCIA

Carrer de Verdi
Gràcia ⑪
www.festamajor
degracia.cat

Life in Barcelona tends to be lived on the streets a lot. Every neighbourhood worth its salt has its own street fiesta, but the one in Gràcia takes the cake. It takes place in August and lasts for two weeks. A dozen streets get decorated with an insane amount of creativity.

157 FESTA MAJOR DEL POBLE SEC

Poble Sec/Montjuïc ⑥
festamajor.poblesec.org

The Poble Sec street fiesta has fewer decorations than the one in Gràcia and more of a student party atmosphere, but it's so very energizing.

158 FESTIVAL DE LA MERCÈ

El Gòtic ②
lameva.barcelona.cat/
merce/en/

This annual festival near the end of September, in honour of the Virgin Mary, mainly takes place around Via Laetana in El Gótic and the Born. It includes giants, *correfocs* (dancing devils with fireworks) and an artistic projection on the façades of Plaça Sant Jaume.

159 SANT JORDI/ ST GEORGE DAY

On the day of Catalonia's patron saint, Sant Jordi, men used to give their wife roses, while the women used to buy books for their spouse. Nowadays those traditions have faded away a bit, but it's still a hugely important festival. The inner city is saturated with writers autographing their work in the street, and roses are sold everywhere.

160 FERIA DE ABRIL
**Plaça del Fòrum
Poblenou ⑤**
www.cac.es

The Feria de Abril (April Fair) actually is a tradition of the Southern regions in Spain, and it's very popular with people from that area living in Barcelona. The festival grounds are located on the terrains of the Forum, where pop-up restaurants offer local food. At least half of the ladies present are dressed in exuberant flamenco-outfits.

156 FESTA MAJOR DE GRÀCIA

65 PLACES TO SHOP

———

5 *fashionable*
BOUTIQUES FOR WOMEN

---

161 COMO AGUA DE MAYO

C/ de l' Argenteria 43
Born ③
+34 (0)93 310 64 41
*www.comoagua
demayo.com*

Hip, fashionable and high quality women's clothing by brands such as Masscob. All items are one of a kind and the store is known for having the finger on the pulse. They also sell shoes (for example Chie Mihara), handbags and accessories. *Como agua de mayo* translates as 'like a breath of fresh air'. Sounds about right.

162 COTTON VINTAGE

C/ de Laforja 96
Gràcia ⑪
+34 (0)93 184 37 40
www.cottonvintage.es

Second-hand luxury clothing (and accessories), sometimes as much as 20 years old. If you read Spanish, check out their blog first: they love to write about luxury, fashion and glamour and they do it well. *https://cottonvintage.wordpress.com*

163 MISTY ROSE

C/ de Provença 333
Dret de l'Eixample ⑩
+34 (0)93 476 22 08

Misty Rose sells urban chic clothing: items you'll want to wear every day that are statement pieces as well. The brands are local as well as international: One Step, Monomi, Juliette Jolie… Become friends with the shop on Facebook first: they post pictures of interesting ensembles on an almost daily basis.

164 CUSTO BARCELONA

C/ de Ferran 36
El Gòtic ②
+34 (0)93 342 66 98
www.custo.com

Angel Custodio Dalmau, owner of Custo Barcelona, may have been one of the first people to realize the commercial value of the word 'Barcelona'. He combined his own name and that of the city, using it to sell clothes with colourful and artistic prints. The 35-year-old brand now has over a hundred stores across the world.

165 LUGGAGE ROOM

Carrer del Carme 5
Raval ①
+34 (0)93 412 00 3

Colourful and fresh, limited collections (by Pitagora, among others) in the style of Desigual. As the name suggests, this store will keep your luggage until you have to go to the airport, so this is a good place to visit on your last day in town.

161 COMO AGUA DE MAYO

5 very
VINTAGE FASHION
shops

166 FLAMINGOS VINTAGE KILO

C/ de Ferlandina 20
Raval ①
+34 (0)93 182 43 87
www.vintagekilo.com

A good rule of thumb for both restaurants and stores is: the fewer items you can buy there, the higher the quality will be. But there are exceptions. Flamingo sells second-hand clothing by the kilo, so you can browse endlessly – and it's dirt cheap, of course. The collection of bridal dresses hanging from the ceiling may give you ideas as well.

167 LE SWING

Carrer del Rec 16
Born ③
+34 (0)93 310 14 49
www.leswingvintage.com

Le Swing pioneered in vintage clothes in the early noughties. These days the shop has two branches: Le Swing in Carrer del Rec has the oldest items, Le Swing Blow in Carrer del Bonaire 6 has the outrageous clothes. Both stores have a wonderful boudoir style interior.

168 DANDELION

C/ Joaquín Costa ;35
Raval ①
www.dandelion
segundamano.com

The owners of Dandelion only offer second-hand clothes from Catalonia, whereas most other clothing stores sell items that have been flown across thousands of miles. And they don't call their goods 'vintage', because the term has lost a lot of its meaning: most of what is sold as vintage, is anything but that. A store with a strong philosophy and generous offerings.

169 **PARIS VINTAGE**

C/ del Rosseló 237
Eixample ⑨
www.parisvintagebcn.
tumblr.com

Paris Vintage is the love of French-born Dorian Lebarbier. Leave it to Parisian ladies to find the best of the best, from the careful delicacy of 50s dresses to more flamboyant 80s outings. You just may run into a Balenciaga, Mugler or Givenchy here. Featured in *Vogue España* and boasting an international reputation.

170 **LULLABY**

C/ de la Riera Baixa 22
Raval ①
+34 (0)93 443 08 02

And if you don't have the money for Paris Vintage (see above), there is no shame in going to Lullaby: the best of various time periods, chronologically arranged, just without the fancy labels. Also sells some men's and children's clothing. You can take a break from shopping and go for some tapas at Resolis next door.

168 DANDELION

5 places to buy
STUNNING JEWELLERY

---

171 THE DIAMOND PALACE

C/ de Rivadeneyra 4
El Gòtic ②
+34 (0)93 193 31 21
*www.thediamond
palace.es*

Guess what this store specializes in. The Diamond Palace is a store and a jewellery workshop, spread over two floors, with also several exhibition spaces, plus a lounge bar in the attic. A Walhalla for jewellery lovers. Bring a credit card.

172 ARISTOCRAZY

Carrer del Consell
de Cent 351
Eixample ⑨
+34 (0)93 272 10 65
www.aristocrazy.com

The jewellery you buy from this Passeig de Gràcia store will not go unnoticed. You don't even have to choose from their 'Game of Thrones'-inspired collection, other collections are equally striking. 'Epiphany' for example, with its floral patterns in gold and silver. Or the 'New Age' line, dominated by square tacks in sterling silver.

173 UNO DE 50

Rambla de
Catalunya 84
Eixample ⑨
+34 (0)93 467 37 61
www.unode50.com

Uno de 50, founded in the 1990s, is now an international chain, selling creative Spanish jewellery at democratic prices. They're great at intricately constructed bracelets and other jewellery, mostly silver-coloured. Also sells jewellery for men, as well as some watches.

174 HERITAGE

Carrer de la Palla 27
El Gòtic ②
+34 (0)93 317 85 15
www.heritagebarcelona.
com

This antiques store, all wood and old-fashioned class, specializes in antique fashion and jewellery. There is no telling what you'll find here, but if you want to splash on a 1970 silver hanger, look no further. Heritage also sells antique dresses (Dior, Balenciaga…), but beware: these run into thousands of euros.

175 KOETÀNIA

Carrer de Blai 28
Poble Sec/Montjuïc ⑥
+34 (0)93 329 63 85
www.koetania.com

This company on the verge of international expansion sells jewellery in several price categories: from cheap (about 30 euros) to expensive (500 euros and above). The big extra here is that the customer can look straight into the workplace. Koetània wants to emphasize the human aspect of jewellery, instead of just offering showrooms full of shiny stuff. Approachable, likeable, recommended.

The 5 places to be for
SHOE ADDICTS

―――――

176 HAKEI
Rambla de
Catalunya 77
Eixample ⑨
+34 (0)93 496 15 40
www.hakei.com

This is Hakei's flagship store for Barcelona and you can tell: two floors, equalling 230 square metres of high ceilings, parquet floors and trendy metal racks. Hakei sells clothes but do come here for the shoes.

177 LA MANUAL ALPARGATERA
Carrer d'Avinyó 7
El Gòtic ②
+34 (0)93 301 01 72
www.lamanualal
pargatera.es

Both Pope John Paul II and Salvador Dali enjoyed wearing sandals by La Manual Alpargatera: if that isn't a good sign, what is. Everything is handmade here, and it comes in a bewildering variety. The store, old-fashioned and homely, is worth a visit by itself.

178 NU SABATES
C/ dels Cotoners 14
Born ③
+34 (0)93 268 03 83
www.nusabates.com

Every shoe here is an original, and treated with natural dyes. Californian architect cum shoe designer Rafi Balouzian and his son Ari have their own collection, but you can also talk over a specific design and have it hand-made.

179 ALVAREZ & MOIXONET

Carrer Comercial 17
Born ③
+34 (0)93 206 44 70
www.alvarezmoixonet.
com

Right behind the beautifully renovated Mercat del Born you'll find the store of Alvarez & Moixonet. They sell 'sandshoes': stylish canvas shoes, ideal for the beach. There are seven collections: hippie, hedonist, cosmopolitan, decadent, chic, artist and idealist.

180 BIMBA & LOLA

Passeig de
Gràcia 55-57
Eixample ⑨
+34 (0)93 215 81 88
www.bimbaylola.com

Bimba & Lola sells accessories, bags and jewellery as well, but you should come here for the great selection of shoes, from ballerina shoes to boots that are made to impress. If you don't like what you see at Passeig de Gràcia, it's not a waste of time to try the store in Carrer de Muntaner 356.

178 NU SABATES

5 places to shop for
MEN'S FASHION

---

181 NUDIE JEANS
C/ de Ramon y Cajal 2
Gràcia ⑪
+34 (0)93 284 61 42
www.nudiejeans.com

Nudie Jeans is a repair shop, where old blue jeans are brought 'back to life'. "Repairing is caring" is their motto and the end result is a hip new form for pants with a real timeworn sheen.

182 BOO
C/ de Bonavista 2
Gràcia ⑪
+34 (0)93 368 14 58
www.boobcn.com

Reason to walk in: the funny, slightly western-style interior. Reason to try on some clothes: the fitting-room is a 1920s Barcelona telephone box. Brands include Bleu de Paname, La Paz, Saint James, Penfield, Plectrum and Cheap Monday. Also sells books, perfume (e.g. Musgo Real) and whatever else looks cool.

183 SCOTCH & SODA
C/ del Rosselló 247
Dret de l'Eixample ⑩
+34 (0)93 176 38 25
www.scotch-soda.net

Everyday clothing doesn't have to be throwaway. Forget about H&M and buy your essentials at a place like this. Scotch & Soda is really a Dutch brand but the store has a very Spanish, welcoming feel. Stylish and pleasant.

184 ON LAND

C/ de la Princesa 25
Born ③
+34 (0)93 310 02 11
www.on-land.com

On Land sells clothes for him and her, created by young designers and the owners themselves. Very often the clothes are as minimalist as the store itself. Designer Josep Abril steers away from the conventional. The place to go to add personality to your wardrobe.

185 THE OUTPOST

C/ del Rosselló 281bis
Gràcia ⑪
+34 (0)93 457 71 37
www.theoutpostbcn.com

Summer shoes and accessories. Bathing suits and bags. The Outpost welcomes its customers in a 'manly' environment (brownish, lots of wood, very accommodating) and then lays out its many riches: Raf Simons, Issey Miyake, Heschung, Robert Clergerie, WANT Les Essentiels de la Vie, Moscot Sunglasses, Boinas Elosegui, Engeneered Garments... Heaven.

184 ON LAND

5 classy
ACCESSORIES AND BEAUTY *shops*

---

186 LA CHINATA

Carrer dels Angels 20
Raval ①
+34 (0)93 481 69 40
www.lachinata.es

Olive oil, the basis of Mediterranean cooking, is central to La Chinata. Shower gels, skin cream, soap exfoliating creams: everything here has olive oil in it. Of course they also sell premium olive oil in bottles, plus a range of (not necessarily oil-related) gourmet products. The *morcilla* (a type of sausage) paté with extra virgin olive oil is particularly good.

187 GUANTERIA I COMPLEMENTS ALONSO

C/ de Santa Anna 27
El Gòtic ②
+34 (0)93 317 60 85
www.tiendacenter.com

Perfume and gloves have been sold here since the year 1700. Alonso (previously: Manos) is officially protected by the city of Barcelona. It provides a different, more classy consumer experience than just picking up some gloves in a bright new store.

188 AMAPOLA

Travessera de
Gràcia 129
Gràcia ⑪
+34 (0)93 010 62 73
www.amapola
veganshop.com

Amapola creates bio-cosmetics: homemade, based on essential oils and other 100% natural ingredients. Products include hand cream with calendula oil, a Saint John's wort cream to calm burnt skin (a tourist must-have), creams for all skin types and aromatherapy products.

189 BEATRIZ FUREST

Passeig de Gràcia 55
Gràcia ⑪
+34 (0)93 467 39 30
www.beatrizfurest.com

In 1898 Beatriz Furest's ancestors opened their store on Plaça Reial. They sold (and still sell) men's fashion. Beatriz Furest carved out her own niche, 'leather accessories inspired by streetwear' and sells them on enviable Passeig de Gràcia. Elegant, stylish handbags, plus some shoes, wallets, purses, belts and scarves.

190 BIBA

Gran Via de Les Corts
Catalanes 654
Dret de l'Eixample ⑩
+34 (0)93 467 39 30
www.biba.es

Handbags, men's bags, suitcases, backpacks, wallets. If you can keep stuff in it and it isn't Tupperware, then it's probably sold at Biba. There are several stores in Barcelona and it's difficult to say which one is the best. Biba, although an established brand, also pops up at Palo Alto Street Market.

5 *lovely*
ANTIQUES AND
VINTAGE *shops*

191 MUEBLES RAM

C/ de Cartagena 164
Dret de l'Eixample ⑩
+34 (0)93 265 57 80
www.11870.com/pro/
muebles-ram

RAM furniture was originally a props shop for movies and used to only rent its ware; only things they had two pieces of were for sale. Now it welcomes the public to peruse its nostalgia-heavy wares: chrome chairs, 70s tables and sofas, radio sets and lamps.

192 L'ARCA

C/ dels Banyes Nous 20
El Gòtic ②
+34 (0)93 302 15 98
www.larca.es

Trousseaus, sheets, table linens and other antique textiles from the 18th to the 20th century, including antique wedding dresses. The store has its own workspace; there used to be a textile factory at the same location.

193 ANTIQUE BOUTIQUE

Carrer de Sèneca 16
Gràcia ⑪
+34 (0)93 415 86 48
www.antiqueboutique
bcn.com

Antique Boutique likes things in their original shape, sure, but the owners also have their own collection. It features a lot of metal, without turning really industrial. Their 'Juliette Table', for instance, is shiny and new, elegant and with an air of the boudoir about it.

194 AGAINST

Carrer del Comte
d'Urgell 47-51
Sant Antoni ⑦
+34 (0)93 301 54 52
www.againstbcn.com

Against specializes in architect-designed furniture and decorative arts from the mid-20th century. Pieces are sold as near to their original condition as possible. The prices match the store's ambition, which is only logical.

195 OTRANTO

Passeig de Sant
Joan 142
Dret de l'Eixample ⑩
+34 (0)93 207 26 97
www.otranto.es

Otranto salvages the most beautiful pieces from houses that are getting demolished: handrails, toilets, ornamental pieces and even street lamps. If you think that's not going to fit in your hand luggage, you should still visit the store for its incredible collection of mosaic tiles.

191 MUEBLES RAM

5

VINTAGE STORES

with a great selection

---

196 **CARRER DELS TALLERS**

Carrer dels Tallers
Raval ①

This looks like a sneaky way to make this list longer than it should be, but really: there are so many vintage stores in Carrer dels Tallers that the street is worth mentioning by itself. Here you'll find 50s fashion (Retro City, number 47), 60s fashion (Soul, number 15), vinyl (Castelló Records, number 7) and much more.

197 **NEUKÖLN**

Carrer de les Basses
de Sant Pere 22
Born ③
+34 (0)93 319 24 12
www.neukoln.es

The owners of Neuköln regularly visit Germany, Hungary and other former Soviet Union countries, looking for furniture that has stood the test of time. What is so great about the furniture here is that you may recognize it, and imagine it in over-stuffed living rooms. But because it's taken out of context, all of a sudden you can see it's ready for years of beauty.

198 GIDLÖÖF

Passatge Mercantil 1
Born ③
+34 627 42 88 77
www.gidloof.com

Scandinavian furniture from the 1940s and 1950s: tables, rugs, chairs, cupboards and assorted items. Even if you're worried Ryanair will charge you extra for that three-person couch, and therefore not looking to buy, a visit to this store is a pleasant experience. There's something about the old-fashioned delicacy of these objects... The place has been redesigned in December 2016.

199 MUSIC WORLD

C/ del Rosselló 201
Eixample ⑨
+34 (0)93 218 22 84
www.discosmusicworld.com

Music World sells the real thing: second-hand vinyl from the 'times of yore'. The extravert owner of this tiny store loves to recommend stuff. If you're a vinyl enthusiast, head to Disco 100 as well: this record store in Gràcia (Carrer Escorial 33) used to sell CD's and a bit of vinyl, but now the focus is on the very impressive vinyl collection, in any genre.

200 VALNOT

C/ de Viladomat 30
Sant Antoni ⑦
+34 (0)93 531 41 79
www.valnot.es

A furniture workshop and store in one, so if the current condition of a piece doesn't meet your demands, the owner can work on it for you. In fact you can even do that yourself, at Valnot's workshop. Apart from recycled 60s and 70s furniture, Valnot also sells china, cutlery and a bit of art. It isn't a big store, but what little there is to see is worth all of your attention; you'll admire it all the more. Check the website first.

5 exciting

DESIGN SHOPS

---

201 GOTHAM

Carrer del Lleo 28
Raval ①
+34 687 04 08 06
www.gotham-bcn.com

After more than 20 years, Gotham has become a reference. The store sells furniture, lamps and a collection of delightful miscellanea. Pricey? Yes. Worth it? Yes!

202 KING KONG DESIGN

Passatge Masoliver 3
Poblenou ⑤
+34 644 04 52 08
www.kingkong
design.com

King Kong sells original designs with 'folding' as the common denominator. Think lamps, boxes and objects that look outlandish and clever at the same time. Extra reason to come here: the lovely little cobble-stoned street it's located in. It reminds the passer-by of Poblenou's industrial history.

203 OBJETO DE DESEO

Carrer de Balmes 237
Gràcia ⑪
+34 (0)93 415 72 82
www.objetodedeso.es

Forget about the old-fashioned souvenir shop and check out this self-proclaimed curiosity store. Vases, odd wall decorations, figurines and other objects quivering on the verge of art and occasionally a larger object.

204 ZABRISKIE OUTLET

C/ de Mallorca 198
Eixample ⑨
+34 (0)93 323 12 47

Zabriskie is named after the movie *Zabriskie Point*, Antonioni's critique of consumerism. The owners of this shop certainly have a sense of humour, because Zabriskie is an outlet, bringing together the crumbs that fell of consumerism's table. Lots of very cheap clothes, picture frames, candles and knickknacks.

205 L'APPARTEMENT

C/ d'Enric Granados 44
Eixample ⑨
+34 (0)93 452 29 04
www.lappartement.es

L'appartement sells some vintage furniture, but it's the quirky stuff they sell that gives this shop its charachter. A bird's nest to keep your keys in and some beautiful candle holders, a pendulum that helps you make decisions and a book-shaped lamp: there are plenty of surprises here.

201 GOTHAM

5 memorable
BOOKSTORES

―――――

206 LA CENTRAL

C/ de Mallorca 237
Eixample ⑨
+34 900 802 109
www.lacentral.com

There are several La Central stores across town, but we're recommending this one because of its pleasant cafe upstairs, with a terrace and excellent pastries. The ground floor has a more than decent English literature section. All the other sections (art, philosophy, science, history...) will have a fair selection of English-language books scattered among the Spanish ones, so do browse: La Central is the most complete bookstore in town.

207 FREAKS

Carrer d'Alí Bei 10
Dret de l'Eixample ⑩
+34 (0)93 265 80 05
www.freaks-books.com

Three stores for the price of one. From left to right: a store with books on movies plus a collection of black & white and weird movies; a comic book and graphic novel store; and a bookstore about every thinkable kind of design and the art of tattoos.

206 LA CENTRAL

208 LAIE CCCB

C/ de Montalegre 5
Raval ①
+34 (0)93 481 38 86
www.laie.es/cccb

The Centre for Contemporary Culture has a singular bookstore: it specializes in art, philosophy, graphic novels and hard-to-find magazines. Don't buy novels here: the literature section is too small for that. You can also find dozens, possibly hundreds of quirky items here, from robot penholders to an ice cube mould that produces ice cubes in the shape of 80s videogame characters. Highbrow and quirky, all in one.

209 TAIFA

Carrer de Verdi 12
Gràcia ⑪
+34 (0)93 217 66 21
www.taifallibres.com

This Gràcia bookstore is located almost right next to Cinema Verdi, which explains why it has so many books about movies and, to a lesser degree, about theatre. There's a big selection of Spanish-language literature in affordable pockets and a second-hand section in the back. Loveable.

210 COME IN – LIBRERIA INGLESA

C/ de Balmes 129bis
Eixample ⑨
+34 (0)93 453 12 04
www.libreriainglesa.
com

Best English bookstore in town (not that there's a lot of competition in that field), with literature, art, children's books, teaching books, dictionaries and board games.

The 5 most colourful
FLOWER SHOPS
AND MARKETS

---

211 **FLORS CAROLINA**
IN FRONT OF:
Les Rambles 91
Raval ①

There are several flower stalls all along the Ramblas – in the 19th century the Rambla de les Flors was the only place in town where flowers were sold – but many of those stands these days sell their wares at inflated prices. If the romance of the Ramblas drives you towards buying flowers, aim for Flors Carolina. Five generations of florists worked in this stand and they only sell flowers, no souvenirs or other kitsch.

212 **AU NOM DE LA ROSE**
Carrer de València 203
Eixample ⑨
+34 (0)93 451 16 50
www.aunomdelarose.es

As the name suggests, Au nom de la rose sells roses. Individual ones or bouquets, common and rare varieties. They also sell rose-flavoured marmalades and sweets, as well as scented candles.

213 **ANNABEL FLORISTERÍA**
Carrer d'Astúries 13
Gràcia ⑪
+34 (0)93 237 09 40
www.annabel floristeria.es

There are two flower shops in this lively shopping street. Floristería i complements (at nr 16) sells lots of small plants and pick-me-ups, but it's Annabel Floristería that takes the prize, with beautiful arrangements, a collection of small fruit trees and everything you need to decorate your terrace for a summer stay.

---

214 **FLORISTERIAS NAVARRO**

C/ de València 320
Dret de l'Eixample ⑩
+34 (0)93 457 40 99
*www.floristerias
navarro.com*

Flores Navarro is a no-brainer. They have got a good reputation, beautiful bouquets and a knack for bonsai trees. Moreover, the store is enormous: cross Carrer del Bruc and you'll notice there's more of Navarro's beautiful flower world across the street.

215 **MARIA PONSA FLORS**

Rambla de
Catalunya 124
Eixample ⑨
+34 (0)93 218 67 81

Maria Ponsa Flors is slowly taking over the little square in front of the store: half of what they sell is on shelves and trolleys in the street, sheltered from the sun by a roof of passion flowers. There's a large selection of tasteful dried flower compositions inside. If you want to start gardening by fen shui principles, Maria Ponsa knows all about that.

214 FLORISTERIAS NAVARRO

The 5
OLDEST STORES
in town

---

216 **GALLISSA**
Carrer del Cardenal
Casañas 5
El Gòtic ②
+34 (0)93 302 69 87
www.gallissa.com

The city council of Barcelona not only protects a number of very old and beautiful bars from being altered or demolished, they have taken a couple of stores under their wings as well. This means these stores are protected against the exponentially rising rents in tourist areas, etcetera. Gallissa is one of them. The store produces 'art in wax', namely a stunning variety in candles.

217 **CASA GISPERT**
Carrer dels
Sombrerers 23
Born ③
+34 (0)93 319 75 35
www.casagispert.com

If you've only ever eaten nuts or dried fruit from the supermarket, this place is going to change your life. Casa Gispert has its own oven (in the back of the store) and exports nuts around the globe. They are tasty beyond belief. Try 100 grams of dread apricots, or the macadamia nuts, enjoy them outside in the sun, then see if you can resist going back for more.

217 CASA GISPERT

218 GANIVETERIA ROCA

Plaça del Pi 3
El Gòtic ②
+34 (0)93 302 12 41
www.ganiveteriaroca.
cat

Ganivet is Catalan for 'knife'. If you're looking for a great kitchen knife, this store is where you should go. They also sell other kitchen utensils, manicure and pedicure utensils, and more. The store has its own workshop. The interior takes you right back to 1911, when the store was founded.

219 FARMACIA GALUP

C/ de Pau Claris 83
Dret de l'Eixample ⑩
+34 (0)93 317 72 83

Several of the stores that are protected by the city of Barcelona are pharmacies, which makes sense: people like being healthy. Farmacia Galup offers a wonderful example of a historic shop interior: on the walls of this 1927 pharmacy you can still see the ads for Galup products. Probably the fastest way to pick up a new toothbrush and some art at the same time.

220 CASA BEETHOVEN

Les Rambles 97
Raval ①
+34 (0)93 301 48 26
www.casabeethoven.com

Pushed into a corner next to cultural institute La Virreina, this shoebox store, open since 1880, sells sheet music, classical music on vinyl and some gift articles (e.g. music boxes). A lovely store for browsing.

5
GREAT MARKETS
where you can find more than just food

---

221 MERCAT DEL BORN

Plaça Comercial 12
Born ③
www.mercatdelborn.org

The Born Market used to be just that: the place where the residents of Born neighbourhood went for fresh food. When the renovation started it was supposed to become a centre of gastronomy, filled with delicatessen. This plan changed when ruins of the medieval city were discovered. Those ruins are on display now, with a small museum about the War of Succession alongside them, plus a couple of cafes and stores. Beautiful on the outside, surprising on the inside.

222 MERCAT DE LA CONCEPCIÓ

C/ d' Aragó 313-317
Dret de l'Eixample ⑩
+34 (0)675 69 36 16
www.laconcepcio.cat

A handsome building, housing a regular food market but mainly known as the flower market of Barcelona. Don't buy flowers on the Ramblas; if you're looking for flowers, plants or seed, this is the place to be. The Conception Market is the work of architect Antoni Rovira i Trias.

223 MERCAT ALTERNATIU PER A JOVES

Carrer de la Riera
Baixa 1
Raval ①

The Alternative Market is a second-hand market in lively Raval and is always good fun. Clothes and comics, tapas and tattoos, jackets and independent design... – you could call this the hipster market. Open every Saturday from 11 am to 8.30 pm.

224 ENCANTS

Carrer de los
Castillejos 158
Poblenou ⑤
+34 (0)93 246 30 30
www.encantsbcn.com

There's very little you can't find at Encants. Furniture, clothes, batteries, books, cleaning products, it's all here. You can buy a beautiful old cappuccino machine as well as cheap furniture. Open every Monday, Wednesday and Friday. If you come between 7 and 9 am you can take part in the antiques auction.

225 PALO ALTO STREET MARKET

C/ dels Pellaires 30
Poblenou ⑤
+34 (0)93 159 66 70
www.paloaltomarket.
com

Palo Alto is a monthly event that proudly presents itself as the creativity market. It's a flea market where you'll find design as well as biological products, clothes as well as art. It has become very popular very fast. Check the website for dates.

PARC DE LA CIUTADELLA

110 PLACES
TO DISCOVER
BARCELONA

The 5 best ways to
GET AROUND

---

226 METRO
www.metrobarcelona.es

Barcelona has an excellent metro: fast, reliable and cheap. Buy a T-10, a ticket that will get you on the metro ten times for 9,95 euro. On weekdays the metro closes at midnight. On Fridays it closes at 2 am, Saturday night it just keeps going.

227 TAXI
www.radiotaxi033.com

Taxis are everywhere in Barcelona. Just go out in the street and hail one. Or use the Hailo app to order one. Rates are low, compared to neighbouring European countries. Be nice and leave the driver a tip, or at least the change. Competition is fierce these days.

228 BIKE
www.barcelona rentabike.com

Barcelona is not the most bike-friendly place in the world (see above: taxis are everywhere) but discovering the city can involve a lot of walking, so sometimes renting a bike can save you quite some time. Unfortunately the Bicing bikes you see everywhere in the street are for locals only.

229 GOCAR

Passeig de Pujades 7
Born ③
+34 (0)93 269 17 93
www.gocartours.es

This small yellow electric car that you drive yourself may not be the coolest form of transport, but the GPS leads you to the major tourist attractions, while talking your ear off about them.

230 BUS TURÍSTIC

www.barcelona
busturistic.cat

The Bus Turístic is the official Barcelona tourist bus. If you're new in town, this is great way to orientate yourself, get a quick look at the essentials and find out where to go later. The Bus Turístic has three routes; you can hop on or off at any of its 44 stops.

229 GOCAR

226 METRO

The 5 best
OUT-OF-THE-BOX
sights close to the Ramblas

---

231 ANATOMIC THEATRE
Carrer del Carme 47
Raval ①

This stunning anatomical amphitheatre is where students of medicine used to watch as their teachers cut into human bodies, spread out on the marble slab in the middle. This neo-classicist space with baroque flourishes served all through the 18th century. Only open on Wednesdays, between 10 and 12 am. Admission is free.

232 BETLEM CHURCH
Carrer del Carme 2
Raval ①

The Church of Bethlehem boasts a baroque façade (from 1681), which is rare in Barcelona. The interior however was destroyed during the Civil War. The church is quite popular around Christmas time because of its traditional nativity scenes.

233 ANTIGUA CASA FIGUERAS
Les Rambles 83
Raval ①

Located halfway down the Ramblas, this former pasta factory was built in 1820 and decorated by modernist artist Antoni Ros i Güell in 1902. It's as heavily decorated as a wedding cake, only with mosaics, wrought iron and stained glass. Look for the plaque in the pavement with symbols of various trades.

234 CORTE INGLÉS TERRACE

Plaça de Catalunya 14
Eixample ⑩
+34 (0)902 22 44 11
www.elcorteingles.es

There's really no reason to be at Plaça de Catalunya, except when Barça is celebrating a victory. If you want to get a good sense of the square, you'd better visit the El Corte Inglés department store. The cafeteria on the top floor used to be hilariously outdated, but in 2016 it had a makeover and now it's a delicatessen bar. The view is as great as ever.

235 PLAÇA DEL BONSUCCÉS 6

Plaça del
Bonsuccés 6
Raval ①

The Ramblas can get very crowded. If your agoraphobia kicks in, it's good to know that you only have to turn the corner to find this adorable little square. It's a good place to sit down and relax.

231 ANATOMIC THEATRE

5
NOT-SO-SECRET
but must-see SECRETS

---

236 SAGRADA FAMILIA

C/ de Mallorca 401
Dret de l'Eixample ⑩
+34 (0)93 208 04 14
*www.sagradafamilia.
org*

The insane architecture of the Sagrada Familia was always worth a quick stop, but now that the church's interior is finally finished, any visitor should brave the crowd and visit this fairytale cathedral.

237 PARC GÜELL

Carrer d'Olot s/n
Gràcia ⑪
www.parkguell.cat

Once upon a time there laid a rocky hill without any vegetation to speak off. Nowadays that hill, Muntanya Pelada ('Bare Mountain'), is Parc Güell, a public park with some of Antoni Gaudí's best work. Geometry and organic shapes melt into enchanting architecture and sculptures.

238 LA PEDRERA/ CASA MILÀ

C/ de Provença 261
Eixample ⑨
+34 (0)902 20 21 38
www.lapedrera.com

Commissioned in 1906 by businessman Pere Milà i Camps, Antoni Gaudí's apartment building is immediately recognizable, thanks to its undulating terraces and roof decorations. Since 1984 it is a UNESCO World Heritage Site.

239 BOQUERIA MARKET

Les Rambles 91
Raval ①
+34 (0)93 318 25 84
www.boqueria.info

The first mention of the Boqueria market in Barcelona dates from 1217, when tables were installed near the old city gate to sell meat. The current structure was built in 1840, under the direction of the architect Mas Vilà. It's a magnificent market. Just try and walk in there without buying some fresh fruit.

240 HOSPITAL DE LA SANTA CREU I SANT PAU

C/ de Sant Quintí 89
Gràcia ⑫
+34 (0)93 291 90 00
www.santpau.es

One of the city's architectural highlights, just five minutes away from the Sagrada Familia: the original buildings of the Sant Pau Hospital. Designed by modernist architect Lluís Domènech i Montaner, it gives a good idea of what a hospital looked like at the beginning of the 20th century. The greenhouse-like operating rooms alone are worth the price of a ticket. Do take a guided tour.

240 HOSPITAL DE LA SANTA CREU I SANT PAU

The 5 best places for
BARÇA-FANS

---

241 CAMP NOU
Carrer d'Arístides
Maillol s/n
Les Corts ⑧
+34 (0)90 218 99 00
www.fcbarcelona.es

Arguably the world's best soccer team, Barça may very well be one of the reasons why you're visiting Barcelona in the first place. In which case a stop at Camp Nou, the 93.000-seat stadium where Barça has played since 1957, is obligatory. You can watch a game in the stadium (see the website), although it's also a lot of fun to watch a Barça game in a bar somewhere in town.

242 FCB MUSEUM
C/ d'Arístides Maillol
Les Corts ⑧
+34 (0)90 218 99 00
www.fcbarcelona.com

Camp Nou also houses a Barça museum, exploring the club's history as well as the entire culture surrounding it. A visit to the museum is included in the stadium tour.

243 PLAÇA DE CATALUNYA
Eixample ⑩

Plaça de Catalunya is a square of limited architectural or historical importance. But if you're in town when Barça has won a game, this is where you go to party: all FC Barcelona's victories are celebrated here, more precisely at Font de Canaletes (the beaker-like fountain). The square is 50.000 square metres wide, so expect a crowd.

244 FCBOTIGA RONDA UNIVERSITAT

Ronda de la
Universitat / Plaça
de Catalunya
Eixample ⑨
+34 (0)93 318 64 77
www.fcbarcelona.com

The biggest Barça merchandising store is at the stadium itself (take access 9 and behold two floors and 2.000 square feet of soccer goodies), but if you don't make it there and you're dying for some Barça stuff anyway, there's a very good one in the city centre as well.

245 SANT ANDREU DEL PALOMAR CHURCH MURALS

Carrer del Pont 3
Sant Andreu
+34 (0)93 345 09 59
www.santandreu.com

In 1956, local artist Josep Verdaguer was asked to decorate the façades of the Andreu del Palomar church with biblical images in a baroque style. He ignored the stylistic request and filled the biblical images with faces of people who lived nearby. In the mural representing purgatory, one of the unhappy sinners is wearing a Barça scarf.

244 FCBOTIGA RONDA UNIVERSITAT

5 interesting
OLYMPICS-RELATED
places

---

246 OLYMPIC STADIUM

Carrer de l'Estadi 52
Poble Sec/Montjuïc ⑥
+34 (0)93 426 20 89
www.estadiolimpic.cat

Estadi Olímpic Lluís Companys, the Olympic Stadium, was built for the 1929 World Fair and received a makeover for the 1992 Summer Olympics that rejuvenated all Barcelona. It was named after a Catalan president who was shot by the Franco regime in the nearby Montjuïc Castle. It's still used occasionally but mainly breathes the splendour of old dreams.

247 PALAU BLAUGRANA

Avinguda de Joan XXIII s/n
Les Corts ⑧
www.fcbarcelona.com/club/facilities-and-services/palau

Blaugrana Palace is where judo, roller hockey and taekwondo competitions used to be held. These days it belongs to Barça and hosts the volleyball games. If you want to visit it, you should hurry: there are plans to build a new Palau Blaugrana.

248 VILA OLÍMPICA

Poblenou ⑤

Vila Olímpica is one of the Summer Olympics biggest gifts to Barcelona. Large parts of the Sant Mari and Poblenou districts were demolished to build the Olympic Village, the streets of which are still named after the countries whose athletes stayed there. The whole neighbourhood looks futuristic.

249 OLYMPIC POOL OF MONTJUÏC

Avinguda de
Miramar 31
Poble Sec/Montjuïc ⑥
+34 (0)93 423 40 41
http://ajuntament.
barcelona.cat/esports/

This pool opened in 1929 and was refurbished in 1955. It was the star of the diving events and the water polo preliminaries in 1992, as well as of the 2003 World Aquatics Championships. The Montjuïc Municipal Pool consists of two pools, a large tribune and offers a stunning panoramic view of the city.

250 OLYMPIC AND SPORTS MUSEUM JOAN ANTONI SAMARANCH

Carrer de l'Estadi 60
Poble Sec/Montjuïc ⑥
+34 (0)93 292 53 79
www.museuolimpic
bcn.cat

This museum, managed by the Barcelona Olympic Foundation, is an interactive space, dedicated to every discipline of sports. The central philosophy is that of the Olympics themselves, promoting values like 'teamwork, work and consistency'.

246 OLYMPIC STADIUM

246 OLYMPIC STADIUM

251 CASTELL DELS TRES DRAGONS

5 *stunning*
MODERNIST MARVELS

---

251 CASTELL DELS TRES DRAGONS

Passeig Picasso 5
Born ③
+34 (0)93 256 22 00

One of the first examples of Barcelona modernism, designed by architect Lluís Domènech i Montaner. It originally served as a restaurant, during the 1888 World Fair. Contemporary detractors claimed that the stern, citadel-like exterior didn't fit the function of the building. That's why they called it the 'Castle of Three Dragons', after a 19th-century drama that was considered kitsch.

252 CASA AMATLLER

Passeig de Gràcia 41
Eixample ⑨
+34 (0)93 216 01 75
www.amatller.org

With two Gaudí buildings and dozens of high-end stores, it's not impossible to overlook the other marvels on Passeig de Gràcia. For starters: Casa Amatller. It was commissioned by the owner of a chocolate factory. References to his last name can be found on the façade: the initial A and almond tree branches (*amatller* is Catalan for 'almond tree').

253 CASA LLEO I MORERA

Passeig de Gràcia 35
Eixample ⑨
+34 (0)93 676 27 33
*www.casalleomorera.
com*

The second overlooked beauty on Passeig de Gràcia is Casa Lleó Morera, a Lluís Domènech i Montaner creation. It must have been amazing living here, with the view of a grand avenue, the coloured glasswork in the dining room and the grand hallways. *Morera* means 'mulberry tree', so look for mulberry tree branches in the decorations here.

254 PALAU MACAYA

Passeig de Sant
Joan 108
Dret de l'Eixample ⑩
+34 (0)93 457 95 31

Casa Mayaca was designed by the same architect responsible for Casa Amattler. The houses were built simultaneously and Josep Puig i Cadafalch went back and forth between the two building sites by bike, which is why the façade shows an image of a cyclist. Have a look at the staircase in the vestibule, with its many floral motives. Casa Macaya is now owned by a bank and is used for art exhibitions.

255 CASA DE LES PUNXES

Avinguda
Diagonal 416
Dret de l'Eixample ⑩
*www.casadelespunxes.
com*

The 'House of the Points' was built for a bourgeois family (the Terrades sisters), but aimed for the grandeur of a Northern-European castle. The text below the ceramic image of Saint Jordi was considered a nationalistic provocation: 'Patron saint of Catalonia, return our freedom to us.' As of late 2016 it is open to the public. The permanent exhibitions focus on architect Puig i Cadafalch and on the legend of Saint Jordi.

5 striking examples of
POST-WAR ARCHITECTURE

---

256 TORRE MARE NOSTRUM

Carrer dels Pinzón 2
Barceloneta ④

Barcelona doesn't just have lots of history to offer, there is plenty of contemporary beauty to be admired as well. For starters: Edifici Gas Natural, also known as the Mare Nostrum Tower. The headquarters of energy company Gas Natural is a skyscraper with horizontal parts jutting out of its vertical spine. The building (completed in 2005) stands within walking distance of Barceloneta beach.

257 CASA CODERCH

Passeig Joan de Borbó 42
Barceloneta ④

This building from 1954 was named after its architect but it's also known as Casa de La Marina. It's possible to overlook it: it stands out in the Passeig de Joan Borbó which is chock-full of tourist restaurants. This apartment building rapidly received acclaim thanks to its elegant look, primarily the result of the blinds all along the façade. Have a peek into the entrance hall; it has paintings by Catalan artist Jaume Guinovart.

260 BIOMEDICAL RESEARCH PARK

258 MEDIA TIC

Carrer de Sancho de
Avila 133
Poblenou ⑤

The façade of Media TIC is subdivided in dozens of triangles, faintly resembling an insect's facet eye. It's located in a brand new neighbourhood within Poblenou called 22@Barcelona, "an innovative district offering modern spaces for the strategic concentration of intensive knowledge-based activities". This is the newest bit of Barcelona.

259 CMT @22

Carrer de Bolívia 56
Poblenou ⑤

Another 22@Barcelona beauty. This building used to be part of a textile factory. It was renovated and encapsulated in a rust-coloured harness. Brand-new but with a tinge of nostalgia.

260 BIOMEDICAL RESEARCH PARK

Carrer del
Dr. Aiguader 88
Barceloneta ④
+34 (0)93 316 00 00
www.prbb.org

The architects of the Biomedical Research Park, right next to Hospital del Mar, didn't have a lot of square metres to work with, so architects Manel Brullet and Albert de Pineda created an elliptical and conical space. The exterior façade doesn't reach the ground, which makes it seem to float. Cutting-edge architecture, right next to the beach.

The 5 best
VIEWPOINTS
to see the city

---

261 CASTILLO DE MONTJUÏC

Carretera de
Montjuïc 66
Poble Sec/Montjuïc ⑥
+34 (0)93 256 44 40
www.bcn.cat/
castelldemontjuic/ca/
welcome.html

This large fortress has a dark history but today it's very much an empty vessel: you can walk through the echoing underpasses, the grassy gardens and overlook the city, the beach and the harbour with its gigantic cruise ships.

262 BUNKERS DEL CARMEL

Carrer del Turó de la
Rovira 61
Gràcia ⑪

The hill known as the Turó de la Rovira offers a 360-degree view of the city. It's the perfect vantage point to overlook all the development and progress that took place on the plain of Barcelona. Originally this area was agricultural land for growing almond trees and vineyards, later it became a sought-after location for summerhouses. City services infrastructures were also built here, such as the Barcelona water company reservoir and the telecommunications aerials that can still be seen today.

265 **ROOFTOP OF SANTA MARIA DEL MAR**

261 **CASTILLO DE MONTJUÏC**

263 MIRADOR DE COLOM

Plaça Portal
de la Pau s/n
Raval ①
+34 (0)93 285 38 32

There's an elevator inside the Columbus Monument, taking you 60 metres higher and offering a 360-degree view of the city and port. Certainly a good way to see the labyrinth-like Gótic district and the Ramblas.

264 TORRE DE COLLSEROLA

Carretera de
Vallvidrera al
Tibidabo s/n
Tibidabo
+34 (0)93 406 93 54
www.torredecollserola.com

This Norman Foster-designed radio tower, built for the 1992 Olympics, has since become an iconic part of the Barcelona skyline. It is open to the public: you can take an elevator to the observation deck (560 metres above sealevel) where you'll have a 360-degree view on Barcelona and the nature on the other side of Collserola Hill.

265 ROOFTOP OF SANTA MARIA DEL MAR

Plaça de Santa Maria 1
Born ③
+34 (0)93 310 23 90
www.santamaria delmarbarcelona.org

If you take a guided tour of the Santa Maria del Mar (which certainly isn't a waste of time), you'll not only get a better look at the rose windows and the marks of the 1428 earthquake, but you will also have the opportunity to go on the roof. Needless to say, the view is priceless.

5
STREETS
you need to discover

---

266 CARRER DEL PARLAMENT
Sant Antoni ⑦

If there's a cool new restaurant or cafe opening in Barcelona, you can bet it's in Sant Antoni and most likely in Carrer del Parlament. Cheap wine at a lively bar (Bodega Vinito, number 27), a restaurant that specializes in potatoes (Crum, number 21) and an arty coffee bar (Café Cometa, number 20): Parlament has it all. Foodies, this is the street to discover.

267 CARRER DE TORRIJOS
Gràcia ⑪

The main artery of Paris-like Gràcia district is Carrer de Verdi, but only a stone's throw away is Carrer Torrijos. It takes you from Abaceria Central Market, past neighbourhood stores (including a great pastry shop, a Mexican deli and several tiny boutiques) to sunny and green Plaça de la Virreina.

268 RAMBLA DE POBLENOU
Poblenou ⑤

Like Poble Sec, Poblenou is a district on the rise: the locals are rediscovering the restaurants, people are moving because they like it instead of because it's cheap – for the time being, at least. This

Rambla is the main artery of Poblenou, a vibrant, beautifully shaded little street.

269 CARRER D'AIGUAFREDA
Gràcia ⑪

'Cold Water Street' is where, back in the late 19th century, Barcelona citizens would go to wash their clothes in the wells and washing areas. It looks a little like Córdoba, with small one-storey houses and lots of flowers. There are several nice shops and bars here, but really the main reason to come is the unspoilt character of the street.

270 CARRER DE JOAQUÍN COSTA
Raval ①

This street leads away from more upmarket districts like Sant Marti and Eixample and injects you right into Raval's bloodstream. Great cocktail bars, seedy phone stores, some odd furniture and design stores and more, all served with that typical Raval atmosphere of youthful vibrancy and hidden poverty. Want the real Barcelona? This is it.

The 5 best
BEACHES
in and close to the city

---

271 NOVA ICÀRIA

Passeig Marítim de la
Nova Icària 77
Barceloneta ④

If you're facing Frank Gehry's *Peix* sculpture (you can't miss it, it's a 56-metre long goldfish), Nova Icària beach is behind you and to the right. This is a family beach, with volley fields and a ping-pong table.

272 MAR BELLA

Passeig Marítim de la
Mar Bella 126
Poblenou ⑤

Again, facing the *Peix*, Mar Bella beach is a ten-minute walk to the right. This is a beach with a younger crowd, mostly gay men but lots of women as well. It's also a nudist zone. Mar Bella and Nova Icària are the best beaches in Barcelona. If you want something else, it's not a bad idea to leave the city; there are beautiful beaches in the vicinity.

273 SITGES

Sitges
www.visitsitges.com

Sitges is the best-known beach right outside Barcelona. This cute coastal village has a seafront almost as long as Barcelona's, the sand is softer and it's usually a couple of degrees hotter than in Barcelona. Sitges' overall picturesque quality will not disappoint, and it's only a 30-minute train-ride away.

274 SANT POL DE MAR

Sant Pol de Mar
www.santpol.cat

A bit further away (65 minutes by train) lies Sant Pol de Mar. You can stay close to the train station and enjoy the bars on the beach, or you can walk a bit further away and lay your towel in between the rocky formations. Great photo opportunities galore.

275 PLAYA NATURAL DEL PRAT

El Prat de Llobregat
www.elprat.cat

Want to go where the locals go? Then go to Playa del Prat. You may recognize the name: your plane landed on Airport El Prat. The airport is close to the beach, but that doesn't bother anyone. The beach consists of 5,5 kilometres of clean blonde sand, with a very mixed crowd. The train-ride from Barcelona to El Prat de Llobregat takes 11 minutes.

272 **MAR BELLA**

5 *lively and beautiful*
PARKS

---

276 PARC DE LA CIUTADELLA
Passeig de Picasso
Born ③

There used to be a citadel here, a much-hated military fortress, meant to keep the rowdy city under control. It was gleefully demolished to make space for the 1888 World Fair, after which this zone became a park. It's big, central and beloved by the locals. The city's zoo is at the far end of the park, and the Catalonian parliament is here as well.

277 CASTELL DE L'ORENETA
C/ de Montevideo 45
Les Corts ⑧
+34 (0)900 226 226
www.bcn.es/
parcsijardins

The city's biggest park, open since 1978. It gets its name from the Oreneta Castle, the ruins of which are still visible in the park. The park borders on Collserola hill, where you can go for longer nature walks.

278 PARC DIAGONAL MAR
Carrer de Llull 362
Poblenou ⑤

The park is surrounded by new skyscrapers, which gives it a bit of a Central Park feeling. The contemporary art sculptures are a bit ridiculous, but the park has a big lake and the beach is close-by.

279 PARC DE LA TAMARITA

Passeig de Sant
Gervasi 37
Tibidabo

Admittedly the Tamarita gardens are a bit further away from the centre, but this is an enchanted place. Only one half of it is designed with classic splendour; the other half is more spontaneous, with nature overgrowing the stones, greenhouses and ruins. To top it off, one of the trees here is a true fossil: the Wollemia Nobilis tree grew on this planet 200 years ago. They grow in Australia these days, but there are just a couple of dozens, and in Europe they're even rarer.

280 ESPAÑA INDUSTRIAL

C/ de Muntadas 37
Poble Sec/Montjuïc ⑥
+34 (0)93 402 70 00

This terrain used to belong to a textile factory, one building of which has remained. The park, rather beautiful, is best known for *The dragon*, a work of art by Basque artist Andrés Nagel.

276 PARC DE LA CIUTADELLA

5 green and relaxing
GARDENS

---

281 PARC DE PEDRALBES

Avinguda Diagonal 686
Les Corts ⑧
+34 (0)93 413 24 00

The Pedralbes Royal Palace used to be the Spanish royal family's residence whenever they visited Barcelona. There's even a bit of Gaudí to be found here: the Hercules Fountain.

282 CAN SENTMENAT GARDENS

Carrer de Can Caralleu 14-16
Tibidabo

In the 19th century, the Catalan aristocracy looked towards France for inspiration. These gardens are one of the few remaining examples. Canals, terraces, ponds, some sculptures and exuberant vegetation make this a must-see.

283 BOTANICAL GARDEN

Carrer del Doctor Font i Quer 2
Poble Sec/Montjuïc ⑥
+34 (0)93 256 41 60
www.jardibotanic.bcn.es

Only half a century ago, a large part of Montjuïc was nothing but a slum. Then came the 1992 Olympics. Part of that slum is now this 14-acre botanical garden. It has plants from Australia, Chili, California, South-Africa and of course the Mediterranean.

284 UNIVERSITAT DE BARCELONA

Gran Via de Les Corts
Catalanes 585
Eixample ⑨

Yes, this is a university building, but don't be shy: just walk in and cross the hall to the gardens. There are several small patios with ponds and orange trees, and a larger garden to the left. Amid the intense activity of Barcelona's centre, this is an oasis of peace.

285 CERVANTES PARK

Avinguda
Diagonal 706
Les Corts ⑧
+34 (0)93 285 38 34

Even though this rose garden bears Cervantes' name, there's nothing here to remind us of the author of *Don Quixot*. However 5 acres of roses (2000 types) should make you forget about Cervantes. This garden is of course particularly beautiful when the roses bloom, in May, June and July.

283 BOTANICAL GARDEN

284 UNIVERSITAT DE BARCELONA

5 impressive **STATUES**
of people, animals and other stuff to look up to

---

286 **RAMÓN BERENGUER**
Plaça de Ramón
Berenguel el Gran
El Gòtic ②

Statues in the street used to be messages from the state to the people, telling them this person or date is Officially Important. Then postmodernism came and killed the idea of 'one history for all'. The 1950 statue of Ramón Berenguer however is an old school statue: a martial figure atop an imposing horse. Ramón Berenguer III (1082-1131) was count of Barcelona and is famous for having fought the Muslim invaders.

287 **SAN JORGE**
Rambla de
Catalunya 126
Eixample ⑨

Saint George fought dragons. Very often he's depicted in the style of the Berenguer statue (see above), but not so on Rambla de Catalunya. Here San Jorge (1987, by Joan Rebull) looks like a boy and even though he's wearing a coat of mail his arms are bare, lending him a more vulnerable touch.

288 FERNANDO BOTERO'S CAT

Rambla del Raval
Raval ①

Gato (1990) by Fernando Botero travelled around a bit from one Barcelona square to another. For now it has found a home in Raval. Large and fat, with a curious smile on its face, this cat is a lot of fun for children to climb on but also a bit unsettling for adults who look at it a bit longer.

289 LADY LIBERTY

Passeig de Sant
Joan 26
Dret de l'Eixample ⑩

Not in the street and maybe therefore even more of a surprise: this Statue of Liberty replica (original by Frédéric-Auguste Bertholdi, 1886) is the *pièce de résistance* of an already quite outlandish entrance hall.

290 IN PRAISE OF WATER

Parc de la Creueta
del Coll
Passeig de la Mare de
Déu del Coll 77
+34 (0)93 402 70 00
Gràcia ⑪

And finally, a statue that struck me as pure sci-fi when I accidentally stumbled into the Parc de la Creueta del Coll a couple of years ago. It's a 54-ton block of concrete hanging from steel cables, and was created by Spanish artist Eduardo Chillida in 1987.

288 FERNANDO BOTERO'S CAT

5 *breathtaking proofs of*
GAUDÍ'S TALENT

291 CASA BATLLÓ

Passeig de Gràcia 43
Dret de l'Eixample ⑩
+34 (0)93 216 03 06
www.casabatllo.es

There are a lot more examples of Gaudí's talent to be found in Barcelona than just the Sagrada Familia and La Pedrera. Casa Battló, almost opposite La Pedrera, blends Saint Georges motives with wavy lines. The building looks organic thanks to the scale-like ornaments.

292 CASA VICENS

Carrer de
les Carolines 18-24
Gràcia ⑪
www.casavicens.org

Casa Vicens (1883-1889) was Gaudí's first major building: a private property in a mixture of styles, including *mudejar* (a Spanish building style with Arab influences) and geometrically arranged tiles.

293 PALAU GÜELL

Carrer Nou de la
Rambla 3-5
Raval ①
+34 (0)93 472 57 75
www.palauguell.cat

This intercity palace, designed by Gaudí for the same industrial who commissioned the Parc Güell, looks surprisingly stark from the outside. Inside it's like a movie set: the dark gray stone, the rib-like columns and the generous use of dark wood give it a decidedly Gothic flavour. Unlike any other of Gaudí's creations, Palau Güell feels alien.

294 EL DRAC, FINCA GÜELL

Avinguda de
Pedralbes 7
Les Corts ⑧
+34 (0)93 317 76 52

More *mudejar* style elements are to be found in the gatehouses of Finca Güell, the estate and manor that Gaudí designed for his pre-eminent Maecenas around 1883. The manor is gone now but the gates are still there, their most famous element being the forged iron flying dragon.

295 COLÒNIA GÜELL

C/ Claudi Güell s/n
Santa Coloma
de Cervelló
+34 (0)93 630 58 07
www.gaudicolonia guell.org

Colònia Güell lies well outside of Barcelona, 23 kilometres to the southwest. It was supposed to become an industrial village with terraced houses, a school, a theatre, shops and a church. Gaudí was commissioned to work on the church. However, after initiating the project in 1890, Eusebi Güell stopped work on the entire project in 1914. The lower nave of Gaudí's church was already finished by that time. The church is now known as Gaudí's crypt and features beautiful vaults in the shape of hyperbolic parabolas.

5
SQUARES
you'll want to see

296 **PLAÇA REIAL**
El Gòtic ②

The Royal Plaza, located close to the Ramblas, is a vast square with a very Spanish vibe about it. Maybe it's due to the palm trees, maybe it's the influence of the bars and nightclubs all around it. The lanterns were designed by Antoni Gaudí.

297 **PLAÇA DE SANT FELIP NERI**
El Gòtic ②

This square, hidden a bit amid the meandering streets of the El Gòtic, was named after the church that dominates it. The church walls show the scars of a nearby bomb explosion from 1938. The bomb killed 40 people, mostly children that had been hiding in the church cellars. Moreover, the entire square used to be a cemetery, back in the Middle Ages. There's a lot of death here, and yet it's a haven of peace in a tourist-heavy zone.

298 PLAÇA DE LA VIRREINA

Gràcia ⑪

When it comes to enjoying a cold drink or an early-morning coffee out in the open, Gràcia district has an abundance of pleasant squares. Plaça de la Virreina is one them. This square is dominated by the Sant Joan church on the one side – very beautiful when the sun finds its façade and produces a dusty golden light – and the Palau de la Virreina (Palace of the Wife of the Viceroy) on the other.

299 PLAÇA DE ROVIRA

Gràcia ⑪

Architect Antoni Rovira i Trias (whose statue on the bench in this square proves to be irresistible to playing children) was born in Gràcia and worked on the urbanisation of Eixample district. The square named after him is a calm place, with plenty of shade in the summer. It is also the location for rock concerts during the Festa major de Gràcia.

300 PLAÇA DE LA VILA DE GRÀCIA

Gràcia ⑪

When Gràcia was still a small village, it attempted to secede, as a form of protest against the conscription of Catalan men to fight for imperial Spain. To punish the village the square was bombarded, but the 1862 clocktower survived. Plaça de la Vila de Gràcia now has so many bars and restaurants, it's on the verge of becoming too touristy, so go and enjoy it now, while school children still play there.

297 PLAÇA DE SANT FELIP NERI

5 important
LANDMARKS

---

301 EL PEIX – FRANK GEHRY

Passeig Marítim de la Barceloneta
Barceloneta ④

This work of art by Canadian-born American architect Frank Gehry is an undisputed highlight of Barceloneta Beach. The gilded stainless steel strips catch the sunlight and transform it into a golden sheen, gliding over the elegant lines of this non-descript *peix* (fish), created in 1992.

302 L'ESTEL FERIT – REBECCA HORN

Passeig Marítim de la Barceloneta
Barceloneta ④

German artist Rebecca Horn wanted to create a memory of the ramshackle beach bars and other constructions along the beach, that were all torn down when the 1992 Summer Olympics swept through the city. Her ode: four twisted cubes, rising about 10 metres, looking fragile and solid at the same time.

302 L'ESTEL FERIT

305 TELECOMMUNICATION TOWER

303 **TORRE AGBAR**

Avinguda
Diagonal 211
Dret de l'Eixample ⑩
+34 (0)93 342 20 00
www.torreagbar.com

This 38-storey skyscraper was designed by Jean Nouvel and built between 1999 and 2004. The tower redefined the entire district around it and thanks to its nightly illumination quickly became a Barcelona landmark.

304 **MIES VAN DER ROHE PAVILLION**

Avinguda Francesc
Ferrer i Guàrdia 7
Poble Sec/Montjuïc ⑥
+34 (0)93 423 40 16
www.miesbcn.com

The German pavilion designed by Ludwig Mies van der Rohe was originally created for the 1929 World Fair. It was so stunning in its Zen-like minimalism that the city soon realized it had made a mistake by tearing it down. So in the 1980s, it was rebuilt, using the original plans and pictures. Try to visit it in the morning: the relative calm on Montjuïc hill and the morning light will make for a lasting memory.

305 **TELE-COMMUNICATION TOWER – SANTIAGO CALATRAVA**

Carrer de l'Estadi
Poble Sec/Montjuïc ⑥

The Telecommunication Tower on Montjuïc was created by the controversial Valencian architect Santiago Calatrava. It looks like an object from a science-fiction movie, and yet if you look closely, you can see it's an athlete holding the Olympic Flame. The tower was built for Telefónica to transmit television coverage of the 1992 Summer Olympics.

5 remains from

WHEN BARCELONA WAS STILL BARCINO

---

306 BARCINO CITY WALLS
Plaça Nova
El Gòtic ②

At various points in the city centre you can see remains of the original Roman walls. You have to know where to look though. On Plaça Nova, close to the Cathedral, look for the two square towers. They date back to the 4th century BC.

307 COLUMNS OF TROY
Plaça de Sant
Jaume 4
El Gòtic ②

The Palau de la Generalitat houses the offices of the Catalonian government. It is one of the few buildings of medieval origin in Europe that still functions as a seat of government. The four columns in front of the entrance are Roman: the marble came all the way from Troy (Turkey) and arrived in Tarraco (currently Tarragona, in Catalonia) in the 2nd century AD.

308 TEMPLO DE AUGUSTO
Carrer del Paradís
El Gòtic ②
+34 (0)93 256 21 22
www.museuhistoria.
bcn.cat/en/node/648

The pillars of the Temple of Emperor Augustus may form the most impressive sight nobody knows is there: they are kept indoors. A sad fate for what was once the centre of the city, the temple of the Forum, as well as its highest point.

309 NECROPOLIS

Plaça Vila de Madrid
El Gòtic ②
+34 (0)93 256 21 00
*www.museuhistoria.
bcn.cat/en/node/649*

Underneath the pavement of Plaça Vila de Madrid is Vía Sepulcral: 70 2nd-century tombs from the Roman necropolis. They were discovered in the 1950s. Partly visible in open air, the exhibition provides information about Roman funeral traditions.

310 UNDERGROUND RUINS

Plaça del Rei
El Gòtic ②
+34 (0)93 256 21 00
*www.museuhistoria.
bcn.cat/en/node/647*

The City History Museum shelters the most extensive underground Roman ruins in the world: 4000 square metres. There are remains of a factory where fish was chopped and salted, a winemaking facility, hot and cold baths for the citizens and pits for dyeing and laundering.

308 TEMPLO DE AUGUSTO

5 places to discover
MEDIEVAL BARCELONA

---

311 SANTA CATERINA MARKET AND CONVENT

Avinguda de
Francesc Cambó 16
Born ③
+34 (0)93 319 57 40
*www.mercat
santacaterina.com*

Since its renovation in 2005, Santa Caterina Market shows part of the remains that were found underneath. In the 13th century, the Dominican monastery of Santa Caterina was built here, which later became the first seat of the city's government, the Consell de Cent. In 1837 it was demolished, an event that helped to awaken the public's romantic interest in Gothic monuments.

312 PLAÇA DEL REI

El Gòtic ②
*www.museuhistoria.
bcn.cat*

This is where the Inquisition burned its victims and where the town's executioner lived. And strangely, there is something oppressive about this square, even though there's nothing ugly about its main building, the Palacio Real Mayor, once the residence of the counts of Barcelona. The stairs in the corner lead to the 14th-century Salón del Tinel, where, it is said, Columbus was welcomed after his return from America. The Salón as well as the Palace's Santa Agata chapel can be visited.

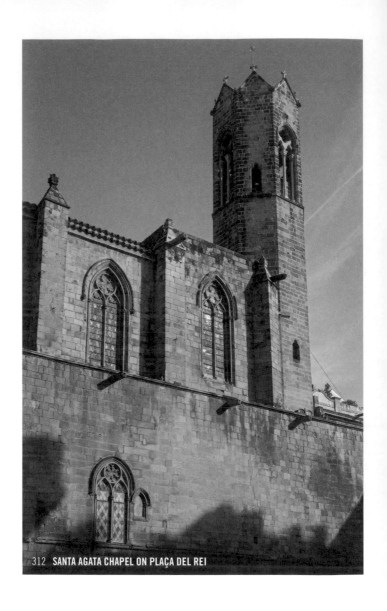

312 SANTA AGATA CHAPEL ON PLAÇA DEL REI

313 BASÍLICA DE LA MERCÈ

Carrer de la Mercè 1
El Gòtic ②
+34 (0)93 315 27 56
*www.basalica
delamerce.cat*

The Basilica of Our Lady of Mercy is a baroque building, erected between 1765 and 1775. Compared to the majestic enormity of the cathedral and the Tim Burton-esque Santa Maria del Mar, this basilica does seem of lesser importance. The most important thing about it is the 14th-century Gothic statue of Our Lady of Mercy, on its roof.

314 BARCELONA CATHEDRAL

Pla de la Seu, s/n
El Gòtic ②
+34 (0)93 315 15 54
www.catedralbcn.org

A Gothic cathedral built (1298-1450) on the foundations of the primitive paleo-Christian basilica and the subsequent Romanesque cathedral. It's big and impressive. Sometimes it's possible to visit the roof as well; it's a movie-like experience. If you've got ten minutes to spare, visit the adjoining Chapel of Saint Lucia.

315 PLAÇA DE SANT JAUME

El Gòtic ②

It's not a surprise this square used to be the heart of medieval Barcelona: when the city was still called Barcino, this is where the Roman Forum was. Today it's still the political centre of Barcelona: on one side of the square we see the palace of the Catalan, opposite it is the town hall.

The 5
JEWISH PLACES
to see in Barcelona

---

316 SINAGOGA MAYOR

Carrer de Marlet 5
El Gòtic ②
+34 (0)93 317 07 90
*www.calldebarcelona.
org*

The 'Call' used to be a Jewish neighbourhood, until the Jews living there were forcibly converted or chased away in the late 14th century. The streets are narrow and the houses seem to lean towards the middle; this is clearly one of the oldest neighbourhoods in the city. The synagogue, a modest but beautiful space, was discovered only a couple of years ago and is now open to the public.

317 CENTRE D'INTERPRETACIÓ DEL CALL

Placeta de Manuel Ribé s/n
El Gòtic ②
+34 (0)93 256 21 22
*www.museuhistoriabcn.
cat/ca/node/195*

Equally recent is the creation of the Call's Information Centre: a small, interactive museum about life in the Call, before it was so dramatically emptied of its inhabitants. It also shows the cultural legacy of the Jewish intellectuals living here.

318 **CALL'S EAST SIDE**

C/ de Sant Honorat
El Gòtic ②

At the end of the street stood one of the access gates to the Call, and in an alley that has now disappeared there were the Font (fountain), the Sinagoga Poca (small synagogue) and other medieval constructions. They now lay beneath the courtyard of Pati dels Tarongers in the Palau de la Generalitat on Plaça Sant Jaume.

319 **REMAINS OF JEWISH GRAVES**

Plaça del Rei s/n
El Gòtic ②

When the Jewish cemetery on Montjuïc was removed in the late 16th century, some of its stones ended up in new buildings in the inner city. Stones with Jewish inscriptions can still be seen in the wall of the Palau del Lloctinent, between the Cathedral and the Plaça del Rei.

320 **NECROPOLIS ON MONTJUÏC**

C/ Mare de la Déu de Port 56-58
Poble Sec/Montjuïc ⑥
www.cbsa.cat

The ancient cemetery on Montjuïc houses the last remains of some of the most notable members of the Jewish community, before the big expulsion. Nonetheless, a lot of time has passed since the big expulsion and what little evidence has been found of the original Jewish cemetery (like the 2001 find of a Jewish headstone, a *matsevah*) has been removed and documented.

5 reasons to visit the
BUSINESS DISTRICT
LES CORTS

321 CARRER D'EVARIST ARNÚS

Les Corts ⑧

A lot of tourists visit Les Corts, but only because that's where Camp Nou is. The rest of this business district seems to go unnoticed. Yet you should at the very least make a stop in Les Corts' standout street, with tiny but beautiful townhouses, an English pub (for the homesick and the beer lovers) and Bangkok Café, Barcelona's only truly authentic Thai restaurant.

322 FARMÀCIA ANTIGA OLLER

Plaça de la
Concordia 3
Les Corts ⑧
+34 (0)93 439 79 05
www.farmaciaoller.com

Plaça de la Concordia is a charming square, dominated by the Santa Maia del Remei bell tower and also boasting the famous Pastry shop Boages. It is home to one of the city's oldest stores; since 1860 four generations of pharmacists have worked here. It brings a bit of tradition and village-like atmosphere to a neighbourhood that was catapulted straight from the 19th into the 21st century.

323 PAU FARINETES STATUE

Plaça de Comas
Les Corts ⑧

Long before Les Corts became an upmarket residential district, it was just a little independent village, the mayor of which was known for hitting the bottle with a certain *gusto*. Even the statue in his honour shows the man in a state of inebriation.

324 PLAÇA DE LES CORTS

Les Corts ⑧

The large buildings you see here? That's where the old Barça soccer field used to be. That stadium, built in 1922, was used until 1957, when Camp Nou was inaugurated. Also look for the small houses with front gardens, highly unusual in Barcelona where just about everyone lives in a flat. They were built in the 1920s for schooled labourers.

325 PEDRALBES MONASTERY

Baixada del
Monestir 9
Les Corts ⑧
+34 (0)93 256 34 34
www.monestir-pedralbes.bcn.cat

The Pedralbes monastery was built in the early 14th century, in white stone (or *pertas albes* in Catalan). Religious art from the 14th to the 20th century is displayed in the monastery's museum, but also the building by itself is worth your time. And apart from works of art, it also exhibits antique furniture and gold and silver work.

5
PALACES
to visit (and briefly feel very rich)

---

326 PALAU MOJA

Carrer de la
Portaferrissa 1
El Gòtic ②
+34 (0)93 316 27 40
www.es.mhcat.cat

This palatial residence, built by the
Marquises of Moja, was designed by the
architect Josep Mas in a late baroque
style, showing the influence of French
neo-classicism. It was completed in 1784.
Notable from this period are the façades
and the Grand Salon.

327 PALAU DE LES HEURES

Passeig de la Vall
d'Hebron 171
Gràcia ⑪

Heures is Catalan for 'ivy'. There's a lot
of that in the gardens surrounding the
late 19th-century, French-looking palace,
sporting four round towers. A beautiful
building, currently owned by the
Universitat de Barcelona. The gardens
are open to the public.

328 PALAU MONTANER

C/ de Mallorca 278
Dret de l'Eixample ⑩

This 1889 palace would look disturbingly
like a shoebox, if it weren't for the
incredible mosaics on the façade, right
under the roof. They represent the
invention of the printing press.

329 PALAU BARÓ DE QUADRAS

Avinguda Diagonal
373
Gràcia ⑪

Despite looking faintly medieval, the palace of the Baron of Quadras was built between 1904 and 1906. Please note the four Gothic-style windows on the second floor and the attic gables. Also don't forget to turn the corner: the back of the house is also worth looking at.

330 PALAU DE LA MÚSICA

Carrer del Palau de
la Música 4-6
Born ③
+34 (0)93 295 72 00
www.palaumusica.cat

From the striking façade to the bright, colourful interior, everything about this building shouts joy. It's a concert hall, built between 1905 and 1908 and created by Lluís Domènech i Montaner. Even if you don't come here for the music, we still recommend taking a guided tour.

5 places you can only
VISIT ON
CORPUS CHRISTI

---

331 REIAL ACADÈMIA DE BONES LLETRES

Carrer del Bisbe
Caçador 3
El Gòtic ②
+34 (0)93 315 00 10
www.boneslletres.cat

The feast of Corpus Christi, celebrated on the Thursday after Trinity Sunday (and thus celebrated on a different day every year), is a good time to be in Barcelona. Several buildings that aren't usually open to the public open their doors on this day, and to top that: for free. First stop: the secluded and charming Royal Academy of Literature.

332 ATENEU BARCELONÉS

Carrer de la Canuda 6
El Gòtic ②
+34 (0)93 343 61 21
www.ateneubcn.org

Today it hosts readings and other cultural events, but originally, the Ateneu Barcelonés building was a private home, which explains the large entry hall (for carriages), the staircase, the elevator... All very chic.

333 PALAU CENTELLES

Baixada de Sant
Miquel 8
El Gòtic ②

This overlooked palace was built in the 13th century. It was a concert hall, a private property and it now belongs to the city council. It looks stern on the outside, but inside you'd swear a wigged and powered French nobleman could walk in any minute.

334 CASA DELS ENTREMESOS

Plaça de les Beates 2
Born ③
+34 (0)93 268 35 31
www.lacasadels entremesos.cat

This cultural centre hosts exhibits about Catalonian folklore. It's also known as 'The Giants Museum', so if you've come with kids and they're sick of looking at buildings: take them here.

335 CAPITANIA GENERAL DE BARCELONA

Plaça de la Mercè
El Gòtic ②

Part of the Corpus Christi tradition is *l'ou com balla*, 'the dancing egg'. It's a hollowed-out egg that is kept in balance on top of the water stream of a fountain. Nobody knows what it means (there are religious as well as secular interpretations), but the tradition dates back to the 15th century. The egg 'dances' in various Corpus Christi buildings, for example in the imposing Capitania General, a building that belongs to the Spanish army.

SANT PAU DEL CAMP MONASTERY

55 PLACES TO ENJOY CULTURE

CATHOLIC BUILDINGS

worth a visit for agnostics

---

336 LA CAPELLA D'EN MARCÚS

**Placeta d'En Marcús
Born ③**

There's more to Catholic Barcelona than the Sagrada Familia or Santa Maria del Mar. This chapel, for instance: dedicated to the Virgin Mary but named after Bernat Marcús, the Greek-Catalan banker who paid for its construction back in the 12th century. It's one of the oldest catholic buildings in town, with a crypt where religious services were held.

337 SANT PAU DEL CAMP MONASTERY

**C/ de Sant Pau 101
Raval ①
+34 (0)93 441 00 01**

This Benedictine monastery was built in the 10th century outside the city walls. It came under attack and was destroyed multiple times, yet it's one of the best-preserved Romanesque buildings in town. It's an oasis of otherworldly calm, amid the buzz of Raval neighbourhood – as if it maintained some of its original, rural charm.

338 SANTA MARIA DEL PI

Plaça del Pi 7
El Gòtic ②
+34 (0)93 318 47 43
www.basilicadelpi.com

A 14th-century Gothic church, the Santa Maria del Pi (Blessed Lady of the Pine Tree, one of the titles of the Virgin Mary) is most notable for its large rose window. Also note the octagonal bell tower and the beautiful alabaster altar.

339 TEMPLO EXPLATORIO DEL SAGRADO CORAZÓN

Cumbre del Tibidabo
Tibidabo
+34 (0)93 417 56 86
www.templotibidabo. info

You know this church, even if you don't realize it: it's the fairytale-like presence on top of Tibidabo Hill (next to the amusement park), shrouded in golden light at night. You saw it from the plane, right before it landed on El Prat. It looks impressively huge on the outside but inside it's mainly details that grab the attention. There's an elevator to the roof, from which point you get a great view of the city.

340 SANT JOSEP DE LA MUNTANYA

Av. del Santuari
de Sant Josep de la
Muntanya 25
Gràcia ⑪
+34 (0)93 284 05 00
www.santuariosanjose. org

This is a church, a convent and a chapel, in neo-Romanic style with modernist elements. The outside is worth a closer look, but the interior won't excite many visitors. The highlight is the painting of the Blessed Petra de San José, by Isabel Guerra, in Spain well-known as 'the painting nun'.

The 5 most happening
MUSIC FESTIVALS

---

341 PRIMAVERA SOUND
www.primaverasound.com

Barcelona is the location of several great music festivals. As far as pop and rock goes, Primavera Sound kicks off the festival season (fittingly, since it's called 'Spring Sound') around the end of May. If you're in town by that time, make sure to check the website: the first concerts are free.

342 SONAR
Poble Sec/Montjuïc ⑥
www.sonar.es

Next up is Sonar, in June. More dance-oriented, less alternative than Primavera Sound. The majority of the concerts take place at venues on or near Montjuïc. In 2016 they welcomed New Order as well as John Grant, Laurent Garnier as well as Hudson Mohawke. A cool festival.

343 FESTIVAL JARDINS DE PEDRALBES

Avinguda Diagonal 686
Les Corts ⑧
www.festivalpedralbes. com

The Festival Jardins de Pedralbes (in June and July) takes place in the beautiful gardens surrounding a palace, which gives it a unique atmosphere, very different from Sonar or Primavera Sound. Pedralbes aims for a more mature audience. In 2016 it featured a symphonic orchestra playing an Indiana Jones soundtrack and concerts by The Cranberries, Tom Jones and Joan Baez.

344 MIRA

C/ de Sant Adrià 20
Sant Andreu
www.mirafestival.com

Mira (Spanish for 'look') searches for crossbreeds between music and visual arts; in fact the visual part of the concert here is just as important as the music. The festival is still young (it was established in 2011) but has been gaining traction. In 2016 it featured Death in Vegas, Tim Hecker and a plethora of vj sets.

345 JAZZ DE BARCELONA

www. barcelonajazzfestival. blogspot.com

Spanish as well as international jazz artists perform at this festival, which will celebrate its 50th anniversary in 2017. In 2016 it welcomed (among others) Asaf Avidan, Bill Frisell, Hiromi, Michel Legrand, Madeleine Peyroux and James Rhodes. It takes place from September through November, at various venues.

The 5 best
CONCERT HALLS

346 EL GRAN TEATRE DEL LICEU

Les Rambles 51-59
Raval ①
+34 (0)93 485 99 00
www.liceubarcelona.cat

The city's opera house, El Gran Teatre del Liceu, has welcomed international singers, musicians and conductors. Lorca and Genet staged their work here. The ticket prices are high and Liceu gets sold out fast. If you don't get in, there's a tour you can take.

347 PALAU DE LA MÚSICA

Carrer de Sant Pere més alt 11
El Gòtic ③
+34 (0)902 442 882
www.palaumusica.cat

Classical and choral music, a Bach series, piano and organ music... Where the Liceu specializes in opera, the Music Palace takes care of all the rest of classical music, plus the occasional jazz and flamenco concert. Every year they have a guest composer and a visual artist who gets a big exhibit.

348 L'AUDITORI

Carrer de Lepant 150
Dret de l'Eixample ⑩
+34 (0)93 247 93 00
www.auditori.cat

L'Auditori is one of those big, bright, somewhat pompous looking concert halls. We would understand people who prefer the Palau de la Música for a venue, but there's nothing wrong with the programming here: symphonic, chamber and early music.

349 MUSEU EUROPEU D'ART MODERN

Carrer de la Barra de
Ferro 5
Born ③
+34 (0)93 319 56 93
www.meam.es

Apart from the big concert halls, some smaller venues are worth checking out as well. The European Museum for Modern Art may sound like an unlikely choice, but this little-known museum offers almost weekly concerts and the programmers have great taste, both in jazz and classical music. You could call this two hidden gems for the price of one.

350 SMALLEST THEATRE IN THE WORLD

C/ de l'Encarnació 25
Gràcia ⑰
+34 (0)93 284 99 20
www.elteatremespetit delmon.com

El Teatre més Petit del Món has no more than 40 seats and claims it's the ideal venue for listening to the chamber music of Chopin, Beethoven and Mozart (as well as the own creations of the theatre's owner, Luis de Arquer). Both the 'hall' and the garden breathe 19th-century refinement.

347 PALAU DE LA MÚSICA

The 5 coolest

MUSIC CLUBS

---

351 RAZZMATAZZ
C/ de Pamplona 88
Poblenou ⑤
+34 (0)93 320 82 00
www.salarazzmatazz.
com

DJ sessions and concerts abound in this huge club. In the five spaces Razzmatazz consists of, you can listen to indie rock, techno, electropop and a handful of genres in between. Every group of note has played here and somehow, Razzmatazz has lost nothing of its cool and popularity.

352 APOLO
Carrer Nou de la
Rambla 113
Poble Sec/Montjuïc ⑥
+34 (0)93 441 40 01
www.sala-apolo.com

It may look like a classic ballroom, but this is Barcelona's best clubbing space. The music choice here is eclectic: from rock over electronic music to folk. Apolo personifies the Barcelona club scene: it's cool, it's now, and it never turns nasty or violent.

353 SIDECAR FACTORY CLUB
Plaça Reial 7
El Gòtic ②
+34 (0)93 302 15 86
www.sidecarfactory
club.com

Like many clubs on Plaça Reial, the dance floor of Sidecar Factory Club lies below ground level. Indie rock rules here. It's not a very big club, which has a great effect on the atmosphere: it feels as if you were crashing a student party.

354 BIKINI

Avinguda
Diagonal 547
Les Corts ⑧
+34 (0)93 322 08 00
www.bikinibcn.com

A Barcelona staple since 1953, Bikini offers concerts (mainly Spanish pop and rock), followed by clubs nights, musically running the gamut from pounding techno to a Bruce Springsteen tribute night. Don't like the music in one room? Move on to the next: this place is big!

355 LUZ DE GAS

C/ de Muntaner 246
Eixample ⑨
+34 (0)93 209 77 11
www.luzdegas.com

This used to be a musical hall. The stage and the archetypal red curtains are still there, only now the stage is used for concerts: blues, jazz, disco, pop, rock and soul, depending on the day of the week. It's a bit heavier on the purse, but for a classy night out, Luz de Gas always delivers.

352 APOLO

The 5 best
ART MUSEUMS

356 MNAC
Palau Nacional,
Parc de Montjuïc
Poble Sec/Montjuïc ⑥
+34 (0)93 622 03 60
www.museu
nacional.cat

The Catalan National Art Museum is the imposing building that tops the Montjuïc Fountains. It has a rather stunning collection of Catalan art, from the medieval period up to modern art and photography. The Romanesque Art, which in Catalonia is much more vivid than in other European countries, is a particularly beautiful treasure.

357 MACBA
Plaça dels Àngels 1
Raval ①
+34 (0)93 412 08 10
www.macba.cat

Originally the only reason for putting a Museum of Modern Art in Raval, was to upgrade the then derelict neighbourhood. The strategy worked. Now Raval boasts an interesting building (by Richard Meier) and a museum with ample space for today's top artists – and the eternal skateboarders in front of the museum prevent it from getting stuffy.

357 **MACBA**

358 CCCB

C/ de Montalegre 5
Raval ①
+34 (0)93 306 41 00
www.cccb.org

A minute away from MACBA, the Centre for Contemporary Culture is a slightly more modest space (although the underground entrance and the staircases can compete with MACBA's design) for thematic exhibitions about science, culture, design, photography, technology and more. It also hosts seminars and has a bookstore with an interesting collection.

359 FUNDACIÓ JOAN MIRÓ

Parc de Montjuïc s/n
Poble Sec/Montjuïc ⑥
+34 (0)93 443 94 70
www.fmirobcn.org

Catalan artist Joan Miró has his own museum on Montjuïc hill. The collection used to be the artist's: 10.000 works, mostly by Miró himself, but also items made by Alexander Calder, Mark Rothko and Marcel Duchamp. This is a major tourist attraction; so expect Mona Lisa-style throngs.

360 MUSEU PICASSO

C/ Montcada 15-23
Born ③
+34 (0)93 256 30 00
www.museupicasso.
bcn.cat

Modesty commands us to say that the Museu Picasso certainly has a fine collection, with works from every single one of Picasso's periods, but that the best-known works are not here: those are in other museums around the world. Still worth a visit though.

5

MUSEUMS OFF
THE BEATEN TRACK

361 FREDERIC MARÈS MUSEUM

Plaça Sant Iu 5
El Gòtic ②
+34 (0)93 256 35 00
www.museumares.
bcn.cat

The Frederic Marès Museum is considered to hold one of Spain's most important collections of sculptures from the 3rd and 4th century. Sculptor Frederic Marès also collected objects from 18th- and 19th-century bourgeois Barcelona: canes, glasses, umbrellas, pipes, toys… If that doesn't pique your curiosity, know that the building used to belong to the Inquisition.

362 ANTONI TÀPIES FOUNDATION

Carrer d'Aragó 255
Eixample ⑨
+34 (0)93 487 03 15
www.fundaciotapies.org

Antoni Tàpies (1923-2012) may not be well-known abroad, in Catalonia he's a celebrity. The Foundation that bears his name is primarily dedicated to his work (obviously) but also shows exhibits of artists from the second half the 20th century. The building, a beautiful modernist creation, is crowned by Tàpies' work *Cloud and Chair*, a whirl of crisscrossing metal.

364 **DESIGN MUSEUM**

363 PERFUME MUSEUM

Passeig de Gràcia 39
Eixample ⑨
+34 (0)93 216 01 21
www.museudelperfum.com

Bit of a misleading name, since the collection consists mainly of perfume bottles. Still, it's very informative on the history of perfume through the ages, plus of course on the bottles they came in. The collection comes in two parts: one is an historical overview and one is dedicated to 'industrialized perfume', i.e. the industry that appeared in the 18th century.

364 DESIGN MUSEUM

Plaça de les Glòries
Catalanes 37
Drct de l'Eixample ⑩
+34 (0)93 256 68 00
www.museudeldisseny.cat

The Design Museum is just a couple of years old and we urge you to go and discover it. It has exhibitions on the four branches of design: space, product, information and fashion. It's housed in a handsome, original piece of architecture, right next to Torre Agbar.

365 SHOE MUSEUM

Plaça de Sant Felip
Neri 5
El Gòtic ②
+34 (0)93 301 45 33

There's 300 years of footwear on display in this one-room-museum. A charming oddity, this one, and it's located on Plaça de Sant Felip Neri, one of the most beautiful squares of El Gòtic, so that makes two reasons to come here.

The 5 most important
ART GALLERIES

---

366 3 PUNTS GALERIA

Carrer d'Enric Granados 21
Eixample ⑨
+34 (0)93 451 23 48
www.3punts.com

The art-lover will find it convenient that in Barcelona so many good galleries can be found in the same street. Walking uphill from Plaça Universitat, Galería 3 Punts is your first stop. Young and established artists get confronted with each other in the shows here (circa seven per year).

367 ADN GALERIA

Carrer d'Enric Granados 49
Eixample ⑨
+34 (0)93 451 00 64
www.adngaleria.com

Next up is adn galeria (that's Spanish for DNA), a gallery with a penchant for socio-politically active young artists. It also wants to be a platform, inviting artists for performances and organizing talks about the links between art and society.

368 GALERIA MARLBOROUGH

Carrer d'Enric Granados 68
Eixample ⑨
+34 (0)93 467 44 54
www.galeria marlborough.com

The Marlborough gallery started in 1946 in London. Now they have galleries in Chile, Florida, Monaco and Barcelona (among other cities). Apart from a cutting-edge collection, they also boast a beautiful presentation place, bright and homely at the same time.

369 GALERIA TRAMA

Carrer de Petritxol 5
El Gòtic ②
+34 (0)93 317 48 77
www.galeriatrama.com

How surprising, to find an art gallery in a street like this – Petritxol is known as 'chocolate street' and tends to be bursting at the seams with tourists. Trama promotes contemporary art by Spanish artists and emerging foreign artists. Created in 1991 and now very well established.

370 EAT MEAT RAW GALLERY

Carrer d'Alzina 20
Gràcia ⑪
+34 (0)93 284 28 94
www.eatmeat.cat

And now for something completely different: this contemporary art gallery exhibits pieces representing 'contemporary realities': "Formal and essential mutations, hybrids, new visual engineering, the soul's sickness, the monstrous, the transgender and the different." One word: dare.

367 ADN GALERIA
COURTESY OF ADN GALLERY AND THE ARTIST ©ROBERTO RUIZ

5 fun
FESTIVALS
for theatre, dance and cinema

371 FESTIVAL GREC

Poble Sec/Montjuïc ⑥
grecfestival.koobin.com

Grec is a yearly international theatre and dance festival which takes place in multiple venues on Montjuïc. Since most theatre-shows in Barcelona are in Catalan, Grec is essential for the theatre-loving visitor. Takes place in July.

372 MERCAT DE LES FLORS

Carrer de Lleida 59
Poble Sec/Montjuïc ⑥
+34 (0)93 426 18 75
www.mercatflors.cat

This is the theatre for all modern dance and choreography in Barcelona. In the course of the year they have various festivals, focusing on (e.g.) flamenco, kids, burgeoning talent and experiments. Tickets can get pricey in Spain; a good idea is to check for bargains on www.atrapalo.com first.

373 SITGES FILM FESTIVAL

Sitges
www.sitgesfilmfestival. com

The foremost international film festival specializing in fantasy and horror films. Sitges Film Festival is a great way to discover the small beach town it's named after, a 20-minute train-ride away from Barcelona. Takes place in October.

374 CINEMA LLIURE A LA PLATJA

Sant Sebastià Beach
Barceloneta ④
www.cinemalliure.com

Free movies by independent filmmakers, every Thursday and Friday, from mid-July to mid-August. Original versions with subtitles.

375 SALA MONTJUÏC

Poble Sec/Montjuïc ⑥
+34 (0)93 302 35 53
www.salamontjuic.org

Sala Montjuïc shows the best of last year's cinema – no blockbusters, but no obscure stuff either. The setting, next to the castle on top of Montjuïc, is amazing. The audience first enjoys a picknick with live music, then a short movie, then the main movie. Very much worth the climb, since the temperature up there is a couple of degrees lower than in the city. Takes place in July.

5 great places the
LOCALS
carved out for themselves

---

376 ALLADA VERMELL FLOWERS
Carrer de l'Allada-Vermell 12
Born ③

Allada Vermell street is nothing but a spacious street in the Born, with lots of bars and terraces. And yet hundreds of visitors have taken a picture of that one house, with a façade full of plants. It's the home of an elderly couple and it evokes a village-like feeling.

377 SUNRISE AT VILA JOANA
Carretera de l'Església 104
Vallvidrera

If you're going to visit the Collserola tower on Tibidabo Hill, go early and have breakfast at the terrace bar overlooking Vila Joana. You'll notice it's full of elderly people, who know there is beauty to be found here in the morning. Apparently sometimes the view includes wild boars and their babies.

378 SUNSET AT BAR DELICIAS
Carrer de Mühlberg 1
Gràcia ⑪

The *delicias* (delicacies) here are a bit on the fatty side (tapas and *patatas bravas*) but the view is great. Locals supposedly come here because the bar plays a role in Juan Marsé's popular 1966 novel *Ultimas tardes con Teresa*. Delicias is a perfect spot to have a bite after a visit to Parc Güell; it's within walking distance.

379 L'AUTOMÀTICA

C/ de la Legalitat 18
Gràcia ⑪
www.lautomatica.org

L'Automàtica is a cultural association formed by artists, designers and illustrators, focusing on endangered trades. In other words: locals keeping the past alive. Central in the workshop is their printing press. Visitors are welcomed.

380 LA CARBONERA

Carrer del Comte d'Urgell/Carrer de Floridablanca
Eixample ⑨

An ugly building occupied by squatters. Nothing unusual in Barcelona, except that this one has an impressive mural. Also, it's the oldest building in Eixample, built in the early days of the city's expansion in the mid-1800s.

380 LA CARBONERA

5 places related to the
BULLFIGHTING CULTURE
(or what's left of it)

---

381 **LAS ARENAS**
Gran Via de les Corts
Catalanes 373-385
Eixample ⑨
+34 (0)93 289 02 44
www.arenasde
barcelona.com

Catalonia has never been big on bullfighting, but these days it's political. Bullfighting = Spanish culture, and this is Catalonia, thus the 'game' was banned by law in 2012. The last bullfights in Las Arenas took place in 1977. The building has been renovated and reopened as a shopping centre in 2010. Do climb to the terrace: the view of Montjuïc is wonderful.

382 **LA MONUMENTAL /**
BULLRING +
BULLFIGHTING
MUSEUM
Gran Via de les Corts
Catalanes 749
Dret de l'Eixample ⑩
+34 (0)93 245 58 03

The last arena to be closed was the Plaza Monumental de Barcelona. The Monumental is architecturally much more interesting than Las Arenas, thanks to its Byzantine and Arab influences. Ironically there's been talk of a sheik wanting to buy it and turn it into a mosque. It houses the Bullfighting Museum.

383 CAN FRAMIS MUSEUM

C/ de Roc Boronat
116-126
Poblenou ⑤
+34 (0)93 320 87 36
*www.fundaciovilacasas.
com/ca/museu/museu-
can-framis-barcelona/*

Can Framis, a factory built at the end of the 18th century, was originally owned by the Framis family. Over the years it fell into disuse. Today, it's a museum of contemporary painting, located in the 22@ district, Barcelona's newly redeveloped technological district. The permanent collection includes a large number of works about bullfighting.

384 TARRACO ARENA PLAÇA

C/ de Mallorca 18
Tarragona
+34 (0)97 721 19 85
wwww.tap.cat

In Tarragona (30 minutes by train from Barcelona) is a very nice arena, now used for concerts, sports events and *castellers*, the latter being a Catalan folklore event where people climb on each other's shoulders, forming a human pyramid.

385 OLOT ARENA

Plaça de toros s/n
Olot

The arena in Olot is the oldest in Catalonia. It's a beautiful building, built with volcanic stone (it lies at the foot of a volcano). There's a bus service from Barcelona to Olot; the trip takes about two hours.

382 LA MONUMENTAL

The 5 best
HISTORY MUSEUMS

386 **MUSEUM OF THE HISTORY OF CATALONIA**
Pla de Pau Vila 3
Barceloneta ④
+34 (0)93 225 47 00
www.en.mhcat.cat

The Museum of the History of Catalonia is housed in what must be Barcelona's most boring building. The exhibitions are nothing like that, though. The parts about the 16th to the 18th century are particularly interesting; they're dedicated to the many border conflicts nobody outside of Spain ever heard of, the rise of the baroque and the technological innovations.

387 **MARITIME MUSEUM**
Avinguda de les Drassanes s/n
Raval ①
+34 (0)93 342 99 20
www.mmb.cat

The Maritime Museum used to be the Drassanes shipyards. Merchant and war ships were built here from the 13th to the 18th century. The highlight of the current collection is a reproduction of a 16th-century galley, next to models, navigational instruments and multimedia displays of life on the ships.

388 MUSEUM OF BARCELONA MODERNISM

Carrer de Balmes 48
Eixample ⑨
+34 (0)93 272 28 96
www.mmbcn.cat

There is a lot of modernist beauty to behold on Barcelona's streets, but maybe you feel the need to have it all put into context. The Museum of Barcelona Modernism has 350 works of art in modernist style on display. It explains what the artists wanted to achieve, where they got their inspiration and introduces the most important names. Very instructive and, of course, beautiful.

389 ARCHAEOLOGY MUSEUM OF CATALONIA

Passeig de Santa Madrona 39
Poble Sec/Montjuïc ⑥
+34 (0)93 423 21 49
www.mac.cat

The Museu d'Arqueologia de Catalunya is actually a group of museums and archaeological sites, including the beautiful Greco-Roman ruins of Empúries. The Barcelona branch has the best archaeological pieces on show, found in Catalonia and its environment. The covered eras include the prehistory, Roman and Iberian times and the era of the Visigoths.

390 ETHNOLOGICAL MUSEUM

Passeig de Santa Madrona 16
Poble Sec/Montjuïc ⑥
+34 (0)93 424 68 07
www.museuetnologic. bcn.es

The Ethnological Museum on Montjuïc recently underwent a complete renovation. Of its huge collection, only 10% is on display. The museum doesn't just want to display items, but it explains how cultures function by putting every object in its context. The number of peoples covered is enormous, so you'd better make some choices before walking in here.

MONTJUÏC AIR SHUTTLE

25 THINGS TO DO WITH CHILDREN

———

5
CHILD-FRIENDLY
restaurants

---

391 CAFÉ MERQUÉN

C/ de Viladomat 36
Sant Antoni ⑦
+34 (0)93 441 47 33

Merquén, named after a Chilian sauce based on roasted peppers, blends Andean and Catalan culinary tastes. So there's sliced *chorrillana* (meat) and tapas, empanadas as well as *butifara* (the Catalan sausage). A welcoming place with decent, sometimes surprising food.

392 PUDDING

C/ de Pau Claris 90
Dret de l'Eixample ⑩
+34 (0)93 676 10 25
*www.pudding
barcelona.com*

The décor is a bit much – it looks like a cross between a cupcake and an enchanted forest – but for the kids there are chalkboards, games and books to keep themselves busy with while the parents can kick back with coffee or tea, a sandwich or some pastry. Inexpensive, bright and ultimately really uplifting.

393 SEMPRONIANA

C/ del Rosselló 148
Eixample ⑨
+34 (0)93 453 18 20
www.semproniana.net

The atmosphere here is homely: part of Semproniana looks like your grand-parents' dining room, part like a kitchen. It's a big space, but strategically placed cupboards with wine and knotted curtains sort of create separate rooms. The kitchen is Catalan with French flourishes.

394 **XIRINGUITO AIGUA**
Jardins del Príncep
de Girona
Gràcia ⑪
+34 648 644 423

A *xiringuito* is a beach bar without walls, just a roof above the sand. There are several such bars along Barcelona's beaches, but Xiringuito Aigua is nowhere near the sea. Instead it's located in Jardins del Príncep de Girona, a park with mostly pine trees. They serve excellent tapas and there's ample space for the kids to run and play.

395 **IDÒ BALEAR**
C/ de Viladomat 43
Sant Antoni ⑦
+34 (0)93 423 96 27
www.idobalear.com

As the name suggests, this delicatessen/restaurant/bakery sells Balearic food – cheeses, meat, wines and other items. They have a children's menu that is as appetizing as it is healthy. It should be able to draw the kids' attention away from the floor-to-ceiling chalkboard in the back.

392 **PUDDING**

5 ways to
GET KIDS MOVING

---

396 MONTJUÏC AIR SHUTTLE

Passeig de Joan
Borbó 88
Barceloneta ④
www.teleferic
demontjuic.cat

The air shuttle was created for the 1929 World Fair, to connect the exhibition on Montjuïc with the beachfront. It fits about 12 people and offers an impressive ride, bridging 1292 metres in 10 minutes, and offering a view of Montjuïc, Barcelona port and the beach. It's convenient and also good fun. Not to be confused with the air shuttle that takes you from Montjuïc metro station to the top of the hill; that's equally convenient but less impressive.

397 FLY AT TIBIDABO AMUSEMENT PARK

Camí de Vallvidrera
al Tibidabo
Tibidabo
+34 (0)93 211 79 42
www.tibidabo.cat

Parc d'Atracciones del Tibidabo is a more than 100-year-old amusement park and funfair with both old-fashioned (the little red plane!) and more modern attractions. Nothing hoary, just a very charming place with a great view of the city.

398 FLOAT IN THE PARC DE LA CIUTADELLA ROWBOATS

Passeig de Picasso
Born ③

There's plenty to see in this park (like the outlandish Castell dels Tres Dragons) but if the kids are tired of walking, why not take them out on the lake, in one of the rowboats? Admission to the park is free, renting a boat costs about 8 euros for half an hour.

399 FLOAT AT BUBBLEPARC

Plaça de l'Odissea
El Gòtic ②
+34 (0)93 309 19 02
www.bubbleparc.com

This self-proclaimed 'micro entertainment park' in the shiny new part of the Barcelona port will exhaust your children. They can safely jump 7 metres high in the BungyDome, walk on water in the Bubblepod or ride the go-cart-like Triketraks. The little ones can steer their very own Acuaboat over shallow water.

400 DRIVE THE GOCAR

Passeig de Pujades 7
Born ③
+34 (0)93 269 17 93
www.gocartours.es

This small yellow electric car that you drive yourself may not be the coolest form of transport, but the GPS leads you to the major tourist attractions, while talking your ear off about them. A perfect kid-sized way of touring the town.

5
WONDERFUL THINGS
to show kids

---

401 MAGIC FOUNTAINS

Plaça Carles Buïgas 1
Poble Sec/Montjuïc ⑥
www.w110.bcn.cat/
portal/site/fontmagica/
menuitem

A water and music show starring all the fountains on Montjuïc. Yes, it's kitschy, the water moving to *Also sprach Zaratustra*, followed by a Queen classic. But you can't deny it's often impressive and the large crowd inevitably gets mesmerized. Different timetables in winter and summer, so do check the website.

402 CHOCOLATE MUSEUM

Carrer del Comerç 36
Born ③
+34 (0)93 268 78 78
www.museuxocolata.cat

Situated right next to a bakery school, this museum will enlighten you on the production process of chocolate, before tempting you with its large chocolate store. Expect to gain more calories than you burn here.

403 CATALUNYA EN MINIATURA

Can Balasch de Baix
Torrelles de Llobregat
+34 (0)93 689 09 60
www.catalunya
enminiatura.com

You'll have to leave town for this one, but Torrelles de Llobregat is not that far away. Paradoxically, this miniature park is one of the biggest in the world: 60.000 square meters of mini Catalonian buildings, including everything by Gaudí, Camp Nou and the amazing Montserrat Mountains.

404 POBLE ESPANYOL

Avinguda Francesc
Ferrer i Guardia 13
Poble Sec/Montjuïc ⑥
+34 (0)93 508 63 00
*www.poble-
espanyol.com*

Built for the 1929 World Fair, Poble
Espanyol is an open-air museum, with
recreations of 117 buildings from around
Spain; basically a condensation of the
entire country. The public liked it so
much it wasn't demolished after the fair.
Over time the museum almost became
an amusement park: concerts take
place here, there are theatre shows and
activities for children, an art gallery, etc.

405 HORTA LABYRINTH

Passeig dels
Castanyers 1
Gràcia ⑪
+34 (0)93 256 44 30

It was once considered the height of
romanticism, but nowadays the 18th-
century Horta Labyrinth Park mostly is
a fun place for children. It's 820 yards
of shrubbery, corridors and dead ends,
leading to a statue of Eros in the middle.
As a parent you can help your children
get there (or afterwards get back out)
because you're standing a bit above the
labyrinth. The gardens as a whole are
beautiful and relaxing as well.

401 MAGIC FOUNTAINS

5 places where
KIDS CAN SEE ANIMALS

---

406 ZOO

Parc de la Cuitadella
Passeig de Picasso s/n
Born ③
+34 (0)90 245 75 45
www.zoobarcelona.cat

The Barcelona Zoo is situated at the far end of the Parc de la Ciutadella. Its highlights are five species of Komodo dragons, the reptile house and the gorilla enclosure, housing seven gorillas plus an exhibition about the species closest to mankind.

407 AQUARIUM

Moll d'Espanya del
Port Vell s/n
El Gòtic ②
+34 (0)93 221 74 74
www.aquariumbcn.com

Six million litres of water are the home of 11.000 fish, including predators like the moray eels. This 1995 aquarium is one of the biggest in the world. The main attraction is the 80-metre long tunnel underneath one of the tanks, taking you up close with the inhabitants.

408 MAMMOTH MUSEUM

Carrer de Montcada 1
Born ③
+34 (0)93 268 85 20
www.museomamut.com

Even though this museum is hidden in the winding streets of the Born, you can't really miss it: there's a mammoth at the entrance. Prehistoric animal skeletons and life-size animal reproductions abound inside. You can touch teeth of a mammoth, feel the horn of a woolly rhinoceros and admire the reproductions of actual cave paintings.

409 MAMMOTH IN THE PARK

Parc de la Ciutadella
Born ③

Another mammoth? Yes, and this time in the wild. The stone mammoth in the Parc de la Ciutadella should have been the first of a series of prehistoric animals, created for the 1888 World Fair, but the death of the artist cut the project short. It looks out of place here, and that adds to the charm.

410 MUSEU BLAU

Plaça Leonardo da Vinci 4-5
Parc del Fòrum
Poblenou ⑤
+34 (0)93 256 60 02
www.museuciencies.cat

The good people at the 'Museum for Natural Sciences' probably realized that the name made the place sound like a punishment, rather than a treat. So it became the 'Blue Museum', after our planet's nickname, and it is indeed a treat: 9.000 square meters of interactive and educational displays about Earth's biography, life in the Mediterranean and the behaviour of various animals.

408 MAMMOTH MUSEUM

The 5 best
MUSEUMS FOR KIDS

---

411 COSMOCAIXA
Carrer d'Isaac
Newton 26
Gràcia ⑪
+34 (0)93 212 60 50
*www.obrasocial.
lacaixa.es*

Formerly known as the Museu de la Ciència, this is a great place to take inquisitive kids. The exhibitions focus on the visually impressive (e.g. an audiovisual spectacle about the CERN particle accelerator), the interactive and the fantastical (e.g. what will human life be like in the year 2100).

412 MUSEUM OF IDEAS AND INVENTIONS (MIBA)
Carrer de la Ciutat 7
El Gòtic ②
+34 (0)93 332 79 30
www.mibamuseum.com

Children are creative and more open to new ideas than adults. MIBA promises to stimulate that creativity. It exhibits inventions, running the gamut from the impressive and the useful (e.g. the vending machine that makes you burn calories before you get your snack) to the absurd (e.g. fluorescent dog food). Good fun.

413 WAX MUSEUM
Passatge de la Banca 7
El Gòtic ②
+34 (0)93 317 26 49
*www.museocerabcn.
com*

Not specifically designed for children but certainly suitable. The Barcelona Wax Museum has the usual historic figures and famous showbiz figures on display, plus Columbus, a group of flamenco dancers and a set of 'fairy woods', filled with imaginary creatures.

414 MAGIC MUSEUM

C/ de les Jonqueres 15
El Gòtic ②
+34 (0)93 319 73 93
*www.elreydelamagia.
com*

El rey de la magia (The king of magic) is a store, a theatre and a museum in one. On Saturdays and Sundays they have magic shows. The price of the ticket also grants access to the museum. The store was opened in 1881; it's now an online store as well.

415 RAILWAY MUSEUM

Plaça Eduard
Maristany s/n
Vilanova i la Geltrù
+34 (0)93 815 84 91
*www.museu
delferrocarril.org*

You'll have to leave town for this one – there's a train going from Sants railway station in the direction of Sants Vicenç de Calders – but if your kid is into trains, it's well worth it. The collection consists of 19th- and 20th-century locomotives and other rolling stock, exhibited in a former station roundhouse and on the surrounding outdoor grounds.

HOTEL BRUMMELL

15 PLACES TO SLEEP

5
HIP HOTELS & HOTELS IN HIP PLACES

---

416 HOTEL PRAKTIK VINOTECA

Carrer de Balmes 51
Eixample ⑨
+34 (0)93 454 50 28
www.hotelpraktikvino-
teca.com

Eixample is heavy on traffic but that shouldn't be a problem when you're staying in one of Hotel Praktik Vinoteca's soundproofed rooms. The hotel employs a wine expert, hence the word 'vinoteca' in its name. Beautiful rooms and a great location: Passeig de Gràcia is close (for shopping), as is Plaça de Catalunya (to catch the bus to the airport).

417 PARS TEATRO HOSTEL

Carrer d'Albareda 12
Poble Sec/Montjuïc ⑥
+34 (0)93 443 94 66
www.teatrohostel.com

Discovering Barcelona on a budget? Try this affordable hostel. You won't have your own room (they only have dormitories) but the service is excellent and the hotel design is quirky and lovable. Poble Sec is an up-and-coming neighbourhood, not too far from the centre and yet not central enough to be noisy.

418 HOTEL BRUMMELL

Nou de la Rambla 174
Poble Sec/Montjuïc ⑥
+34 (0)93 125 86 22
www.hotelbrummell.com

Another hotel in Poble Sec. This boutique hotel has a minimalist design, a sun deck with a small pool, a restaurant (The Box Social) and 20 compact rooms with free Wi-Fi and rainshowers. The penthouse rooms have their own little terrace.

419 BARCELÓ RAVAL

Rambla del Raval
17-21
Raval ①
+34 (0)93 320 14 90
www.barcelo.com/
barcelohotels

This four-star hotel doesn't come cheap, but the experience will be memorable. The purple tower, entirely covered in metal blinds, has been injected into popular Raval district like an alien *Fremdkörper* into a human body. The entrance hall is exuberantly glamorous, the rooms impeccable and the roof terrace provides a 360-degree view of the neighbourhood.

420 BANYS ORIENTALS

C/ de l'Argenteria 37
Born ③
+34 (0)93 268 84 60
www.hotelbanyes
orientals.com

Named after the Arab bathhouse that used to be here, Banyes Orientals is an up-to-date, stylish hotel, with small rooms in simple colours. Located in the Born, which means enormous amounts of tourists during the day but no traffic at night. The number of great restaurants, coffee houses and clothes stores in the immediate vicinity is enormous.

418 HOTEL BRUMMELL

The 5 best
HOTELS BY THE SEA

421 HOTEL PULLMAN SKIPPER

Avinguda
del Litoral 10
Barceloneta ④
+34 (0)93 221 65 65
www.pullman-
barcelona-skipper.com

A sea view tends to come at a cost. Nevertheless, if you can afford it, Barcelona has a couple of hotels that will make it worth the investment. Pullman Barcelona Skipper, for starters: not even a minute away from the beach, right next to an architectural marvel, a rooftop pool with a view of a Barcelona landmark and rooms worthy of a five-star hotel.

422 HOTEL ARTS

C/ de la Marina 19-21
Barceloneta ④
+34 (0)93 221 10 00
www.hotelarts
barcelona.com

Hotel Arts is a 44-storey building by the beach that seems to be wearing a metal harness, consisting of horizontal, vertical and crisscrossing bars. The inside looks just as futuristic. Arts boasts several bars and restaurants, at least two of which (Arola and Enoteca) are outstanding.

423 W BARCELONA

Plaça de la Rosa dels
Vents 1
Barceloneta ④
+34 (0)93 295 28 00
www.w-barcelona.cat

W was built to dazzle. The entrance hall is huge – it sucks your gaze upwards, whether you want to or not. The lounge area, the views…, everything here is XXL. As a pleasant contrast, the rooms go for impeccable minimalism.

424 HILTON DIAGONAL MAR

C/ del Taulat 262-264
Poblenou ⑤
+34 (0)93 507 07 07
www3.hilton.com

A bit further away from the centre, in case you want to avoid the biggest flocks of tourists. Hilton Diagonal Mar is popular among businessmen because the Forum is close-by, but everyone should be able to enjoy the stylish rooms, the Purobeach rooftop pool and sunbathing terrace and the view of famous and less famous landmarks.

425 HOTEL SUBUR

Paseo de la Ribera 66
Sitges
+34 (0)93 894 00 66
www.hotelsubur.com

You may also decide to stay in nearby Sitges and discover Barcelona from there: a little less crowded, about two degrees warmer. In that case Hotel Subur comes highly recommended. Close to the beach and at night postcard-like San Bartolomé Church is within sight.

423   VIEW FROM W BARCELONA

The 5 most
STYLISH B&Bs

426 HOSTAL GOYA

C/ de Pau Claris 74
Dret de l'Eixample ⑩
+34 (0)93 302 26 65
www.hostalgoya.com

The front door to Hostal Goya may not look like much, but the building contains vintage *modernista* decoration. The rooms are crisp and minimalist, so that the original design elements get a chance to stand out.

427 HOSTAL L'ANTIC ESPAI

Gran Via de les Corts
Catalanes 660
Dret de l'Eixample ⑩
+34 (0)93 304 19 45
www.anticespai.com

It's often overlooked, but it's worth knowing that the splendid houses built by the early 20th-century Barcelona bourgeoisie were stuffed to the brink with splendid furniture as well. L'Antic Espai has recreated that experience by filling its rooms with antiques. It feels like spending some time in a treasure trove.

428 POBLENOU BED & BREAKFAST

Carrer del Taulat 30
Poblenou ⑤
+34 (0)93 221 26 01
www.hostalpoblenou.com

A 1930s two-storey house with beautiful façade, handsomely renovated rooms and – this should be the clincher – situated in Poblenou, a neighbourhood that is considered Barcelona's next big surprise. Discover it before everybody else does.

429 PENSION EOS

Gran Via de les Corts
Catalanes 575
Eixample ⑨
+34 (0)93 451 87 72
www.pensioneos.com

This gay-run hostel, close to Plaça Universitat, has interesting murals, a lounge area with a pool table, bright and well-designed rooms and two terraces. No particular design concept, just a very relaxed place smack-dap in the middle of... well, everything.

430 THE 8

Carrer d'Aragó 281
Eixample ⑨
+34 (0)93 676 43 78
www.the8bedand
breakfast.com

THE 8 is a boutique hostel. They really like minimalism here: black and white rule. The whole place is spanking new. Bathrooms come with Rituals products, the breakfast space doubles as a lounge. Carrer Aragó is a really busy street, but the noise is non-existent inside.

428 **POBLENOU BED & BREAKFAST**

ELS ENCANTS VELLS

70 GOOD-TO-KNOW FACTS AND URBAN DETAILS

5
ESSENTIAL DATES
to understand Barcelona's history

---

431 **19 BC**

The Romans conquer the Iberian peninsula, settling the town of Barcino. The settlement is only created to distribute land among retired soldiers. Barcino's location allows for economic development. When Barcino has become Barcelona, the Romans have left behind a Temple of Augustus.

432 **1714**

By the 18th century the various Spanish kingdoms have been unified and are vastly wealthy, thanks to their colonies in the new world. A dispute over the succession of King Charles II leads to the War of the Spanish Succession. Barcelona reluctantly sides with Charles III of Austria and is virtually destroyed by the Bourbon army.

433 **25 JULY-2 AUGUST 1909: SETMANA TRÀGICA**

'Tragic Week': a series of bloody confrontations between the Spanish army and the working classes of Barcelona and other cities of Catalonia, caused by the calling-up of reserve troops to be sent as reinforcements to Morocco, where Spain was fighting the Second Rif War. Circa 150 people died; over 1700 individuals were indicted in military courts for 'armed rebellion'.

434 **1938**

Barcelona bled during the Civil War (1936-1939). The city repeatedly suffered from air raids. Under the command of Mussolini, Italian aircraft bombed the city 13 times, dropping 44 tons of bombs aimed specifically at civilians. More than 1000 people died; over 2000 were injured. General Franco, as a retribution against the Catalan population, had requested these attacks.

435 **1992 SUMMER OLYMPICS**

The Summer Olympics recreated Barcelona as a tourist destination. The city's renovations in the early 90s are still held up as an example for any city hosting the Olympics. Spain lived the dream of an economic boom, a dream that was cut short in 2008 when the economic crisis burst Spain's housing bubble.

The 5 best
HISTORY BOOKS
about Barcelona

---

436 GEORGE ORWELL: HOMAGE TO CATALONIA (1938)

An account of Orwell's experiences in the Spanish Civil War. The author of *1984* and *Animal Farm* arrived in Barcelona in December 1938, with the express aim 'to fight against Fascism'. He joined the POUM, one of the Communist parties, and served on the Aragon front. Orwell returned home with a balanced report of a bloody and confused war.

437 ROBERT HUGHES: BARCELONA (1992)

Initially Robert Hughes was going to write a book about Barcelona's modernism, but it turned into a vast history of the city, from its foundation to the early 20th century. The opening chapters (about the creation of Catalan identity) and the closing chapters (about modernism) are pivotal.

438 **COLM TÓIBÍN: HOMAGE TO BARCELONA (1990)**

Tóibín, a Booker Prize-shortlisted Irish novelist, has lived on and off in Barcelona since the 1970s. In this book he writes about the city's culture and history and foremost about the many changes he has seen it go through in the course of years. Barcelona also features in Tóibín's earlier novel *The South* (1990).

439 **MICHAEL EAUDE: CATALONIA. A CULTURAL HISTORY (2007)**

This book covers roughly the same period of time as Robert Hughes' (much fatter) tome, with more emphasis on Catalonia's position in Spain. The geographical scope is broader, since the subject is all of Catalonia instead of 'just' Barcelona.

440 **NICK LLOYD: FORGOTTEN PLACES. BARCELONA AND THE SPANISH CIVIL WAR (2015)**

In the first part of this highly readable book, Barcelona tour guide Nick Lloyd explains the origins of the Spanish Civil War and introduces the many players on the War's chessboard. The second half is dedicated to the places in Barcelona that played a role during the war. A lively account, thanks to the quotes of people who lived through it all.

5
NOVELS
set in Barcelona

---

441 CARLOS RUÍZ ZAFON: THE SHADOW OF THE WIND (2001)

Think the throngs of tourists make it difficult to see the grandeur of the Ramblas? *The Shadow of the Wind* returns the magic to Barcelona's old city. In Franco-era Spain, a young librarian tries to find out more about mysterious writer Julian Carax, discovering forgotten places in the city in the process. Enjoyable, but don't bother with the sequels.

442 EDUARDO MENDOZA: THE CITY OF MARVELS (1986)

Eduardo Mendoza has been consistently successful with both the readers and the critics ever since his 1975 debut novel. International fame followed in 1986 with this hugely enjoyable novel about a scoundrel's rise to fame in Barcelona between the two World Fairs (1888 and 1929). With its daunting mix of history and fantasy, *The City of Marvels* gives a tongue-in-cheek account of Barcelona's glory years.

443 ILDEFONSO FALCONES: THE CATHEDRAL OF THE SEA (2006)

A story built around the construction of the Santa María del Mar cathedral, by a writer who has clearly done his research about Spain in the 14th century, with its melting pot of Spaniards, Jews and Arabs. Not a literary masterpiece but certainly a good holiday read. Central neighbourhood: Born.

444 ALBERT SÁNCHEZ PIÑOL: VICTUS. THE FALL OF BARCELONA (2012)

Albert Sánchez Piñol couldn't have expected this historical novel to become such a massive bestseller. Now internationally translated, *Victus* takes a dramatic event in Barcelona's history (the city's siege, at the end of the War of Spanish Succession) and turns it into a sweeping sword-and-dagger adventure story. Central neighbourhood: Born.

445 MERCÈ RODODERA: IN DIAMOND SQUARE (1962)

Only recently translated in English, Mercè Rododera's *In Diamond Square* (1962) is a Catalan classic. Poverty and war give dramatic turns to what begins like a straightforward love story. Rododera, influenced by modernist authors, wrote it all in a stream of consciousness style, reminiscent of Virginia Woolf. Central neighbourhood: Gràcia.

The 5 best
MOVIES
shot in Barcelona

---

446 TODO SOBRE MI MADRE (1999)

Pedro Almodóvar's best movie is (coincidentally?) also his only movie shot in Barcelona. A sprawling story, *All About my Mother* features Penelope Cruz as an HIV-positive nun and Carmen Maura as the grieving mother taking care of her.

447 VICKY CRISTINA BARCELONA (2008)

Woody Allen transforms Barcelona in a dream-like place where American women go to confront (and possibly live) their dreams. Light-hearted, yet surprisingly touching.

448 THE PASSENGER (1975)

Partly set and shot in Barcelona, this Michelangelo Antonioni movie stars Jack Nicholson as a journalist who assumes the identity of a deceased hotel guest, in order to start a new life.

449 BARCELONA, ANTES DE QUE EL TIEMPO LO BORRE (2010)

How did Barcelona become a modernist jewel? The answer is: thanks to the enormous wealth that was there at the beginning of the 20th century. This documentary portrays the wealthy bourgeoisie of a booming city, focusing on the director's own family, the Baladías. *Barcelona, Before Time Erases it* is basically *The Great Gatsby* in Spain.

450 BIUTIFUL (2010)

This Mexican-Spanish drama shows a very different side of Barcelona: the poverty of illegal migrants, street vendors and sweatshop employees. Javier Bardem plays a dying man who can't cope with the accident he caused (in which several illegal migrants were killed). A bleak movie, directed by Alejandro González Iñárritu (*Amores Perros*).

5

MUSIC VIDEOS

shot in Barcelona

---

451 KYLIE MINOGUE: SLOW

This 2003 Kylie ditty opens with a beautiful shot of Barcelona seen from the Piscina Municipal de Montjuïc, built for the 1992 Summer Olympics and still in use. The music video is as sexy and languorous as any summer day in Barcelona.

452 SHAKIRA: LOCA

Mainly shot at the Barcelona beaches, *Loca* (2010) shows Shakira doing *loca* (crazy) stuff, as well as the madness that bursts forth when the Columbian pop star is recognized by passers-by.

453 EVANESCENCE: MY IMMORTAL

A 2003 song by American rock band Evanescence. The video shows the band wandering through Born. Plaça de Sant Felip Neri is central, which is fitting since the square shows the scars of Civil War, whereas the lyrics talk about scars that never heal. Atmospheric stuff.

454 **FELIX JAEHN &
JASMINE THOMPSON:
AIN'T NOBODY
(LOVES ME BETTER)**

Hipster beards, coffee to go, skateboards and beautiful young people falling in love: Barcelona has seldom looked more Instagram than this. La Boqueria market makes an appearance. A beachy, bouncy video (2015) that will make you want to move here immediately.

455 **JUSTIN TIMBERLAKE:
SEXY BACK**

Sexy Back (2006) shows Justin Timberlake indulging in some 007 spy shenanigans in a super-cool luxury hotel (unfortunately unidentified) in Barcelona. Shot by Michael Haussman, a director who already knew Spain from his work on Madonna's *Take a Bow*. Starts with a majestic shot of the Montjuïc air shuttle.

5
CATALAN PHRASES
that will make people like you

---

456 BON DIA / BONA TARDA / BONA NIT / ADÉU

It's silly, but speaking the tiniest bit of Catalan will make the locals treat you like a visitor instead of like a tourist. Start off any conversation with these three phrases meaning good morning, good afternoon and good evening. *Adéu* means goodbye.

457 SISPLAU / GRÀCIES

Sisplau, short for *si us plau*, translates as 'as you like it' and means 'please'. *Gràcies*, pronounced the exact same way as Spanish gracias means 'thank you'.

458 PERDONI, QUANT COSTA AIXÒ?

'Excuse me, how much is this?' Hopefully the shopkeeper will answer in English, because an introduction to numbers in Catalan is going to take a while. Whatever he says, *Es una mica car, no?* (That's a bit expensive, isn't it?) is always a good response.

459 EM DIC... SÓC DE... MOLT DE GUST.

'My name is... I'm from... Pleased to meet you'. If your interlocutor takes all this to mean you speak Catalan, your next useful phrase is going to be *No ho entenc. Parla anglès?*: 'I don't understand. Do you speak English?'

460 T'ESTIMO. DEIXA'M EN PAU.

Love comes quickly, so be prepared. *T'estimo* means 'I love you'. Unwanted suitors can be chased off with a harsh *Deixa'm en pau* or 'Leave me in peace'.

5 typical
BARCELONA FOODS

---

461 PATATAS BRAVAS

This dish of deep-fried, roughly cut potatoes served with a spicy tomato sauce can be enjoyed in just about every bar and every restaurant in town. *Bravas* means 'brave' and refers to the hotness of the sauce.

462 PAN AMB TOMÀQUET

Similar to the Italian bruschetta, *pan con tomate* is a slice of baguette, rubbed with a ripe tomato and sprinkled with olive oil and salt. Served as a *tapa* (small entree) or to accompany any dish. In the latter case it should be free.

463 CALÇOTS

A mild-tasting sort of onion, best grilled (on a barbecue) until charred. Once peeled, it gets dipped in *romesco* sauce, a nut and red pepper-based sauce originating from Tarragona (Catalonia). The calçots have their own party, the Calçotada, celebrated in winter both in restaurants and in the streets.

464 ARROZ NEGRO

A paella-like dish, this rice is served with bits of squid and coloured black with the squid's ink. It comes with *aioli* (a garlic-flavoured mayonnaise) and usually some prawns. It's as delicious as it looks striking.

465 CREMA CATALANE

Supposedly a precursor to the better-known French dessert *crème brûlée*. Although they look similar, *crema catalana* mainly consists of milk, whereas *crème brûlée* is cream-based. Cinnamon and lemonpeel further define the taste. It's meant to be eaten on March 19, but you can get it all year round.

5 things to know about
COFFEE
in Spain

---

466 CAFÉ SOLO

What the rest of the world calls an espresso: a tiny bit of extremely strong coffee.

467 CORTADO

What the rest of the world calls a cappuccino, the Spaniards call *café con leche*. However, instead of a big cup of coffee with milk, they prefer the mini-version: the *cortado* (or 'cut'). Usually it is served in a small glass instead of a cup.

468 CAFÉ AMERICANO

A big cup of diluted espresso.

469 CARAJILLO

Usually served in the same small glass the Spaniards use for a *cortado*, the *carajillo* is an espresso, upgraded with a shot of Picardía brandy. For those mornings when just caffeine simply won't do. You can also have it with some milk thrown in the mix; then it's called a *trifásico* and tastes somewhat like Baileys.

470 **CAFÉ CON HIELO** An espresso, served with big chunks of ice. It's a welcome refreshment on a hot day, but don't forget to stir some sugar in the coffee before pouring it over the ice cubes; otherwise the final result will be quite bitter.

CAFÉ SOLO, CAFÉ AMERICANO AND CAFÉ CORTADO

5 *intriguing*
ABANDONED PLACES
and EMPTY SPACES

---

471 GAUDÍ METRO STATION
Plaça de Gaudí
Dret de l'Eixample ⑩

Metro stop Gaudí was built in 1968 but a change in plans regarding the metro lines caused it to never be used. Instead, metro stop Sagrada Familia was inaugurated. If you take the metro from Sagrada Familia to the next stop, Sant Pau/Dos de Maig, you'll see the platforms of the abandoned stop flash by.

472 THE MAIANS ISLAND
Passeig d'Isabel II
Born ③

Walking between the França railway station and Pla del Palau, you're actually walking on an island. Or what used to be an island, until the 15th century, when Barcelona decided it needed a bigger port. The island of Maians, little more than a breakwater used to unload ships, was swallowed by the city.

473 CANÓDROMO
Avinguda
de la Meridiana
Dret de l'Eixample ⑩

Barcelona's Canódrome was the last Spanish greyhound racing circuit to be closed. The building (with its tear-shaped roof and vertical blinds) was too striking to just tear down, so after several other plans failed, it is now set to be a space for the creative industry.

474 PLAÇA DEL FOSSAR DE LES MORERES

Born ③

There is something eerie about this square. It's too empty, compared to the rest of the neighbourhood. The spiky monument and the burning fire don't help. It's all very fitting, since the square used to be a cemetery and the monument keeps the memory alive of the men and women who died during the 1714 siege of Barcelona.

475 ABANDONED HOSPITAL DEL TORAX

Carretera BV-1274
Terrassa

The isolated Hospital del Tórax is where patients suffering from lung cancer, fibrosis and tuberculosis went to get treatment, from the 1950s to 1997. It was said the suicide rate was alarmingly high and satanic rituals were performed in the chapel. In 2004 the police arrested a young man who had stolen a foetus, conserved in formaldehyde, from the dilapidated hospital. Since its closure, three horror films have been shot here.

5 *weird and lavish*
PORTER'S LODGES

---

476 HORSE HEAD
Via Augusta 109
Gràcia ⑪

You shouldn't be shy to peek into the porter's lodges of Barcelona's buildings. It used to be customary to have a porter, who needed a place to sit, as well as space where visitors could wait to get in. Now that the porters have mostly gone, these empty porter's lodges can be hilarious and eerie places. This one is mainly odd, with the black and white marble, the door with forged iron decorations and (of course) the marble horse head.

477 GOTHIC BROTHEL
Via Augusta 159
Gràcia ⑪

There are a lot of good porter's lodges on Via Augusta, but they mostly look like the ones that can be found all over the town, mainly in Eixample. This one however looks like a set for a Gothic fairytale, with its red leather couches and milk glass lights, vainly attacking the darkness.

478 SPACESHIP

Via Augusta 139
Gràcia ⑪

This one is just eerie: a narrow box, reminiscent of the *2001: A Space Odyssey* set. To the left there's a slope towards the basement, producing a creepy light.

479 BRICK ATTACK

Via Augusta 130
Gràcia ⑪

This is the masterpiece. On the right: a wall of bricks, with wooden mailboxes that have clearly become antique. On the left: a square fake-marble table, some couches and a half-moon desk – a cocktail bar. The porter overlooks his domain from a desk on the first floor.

480 NOT QUITE A MIES VAN DER ROHE

Via Augusta 195
Gràcia ⑪

The idea for the green marble wall was clearly stolen from Mr van der Rohe's pavilion on Montjuïc, but sadly the architect didn't copy the minimalism of the pavilion. Instead he went for abundance. Top of the bill: the crystal chandelier in the shape of a goose feather.

5 remains of
VIOLENCE

---

481 GENERAL PRIM'S GRENADE

Carrer de Socrates/
Carrer Gran de Sant
Andreu
Dret de l'Eixample ⑩

Sometimes violence from the past leaves indelible marks. And sometimes those marks are kept in place on purpose. Out of this building's façade sticks something that looks like a breast but it's really a grenade, fired by the governor of the city, who was forced to flee the city after protests against him. It happened on September 22, 1843.

482 THE POISONING OF NAPOLEON'S TROOPS

Carrer d' Ataülf
El Gòtic ②

This pharmacy on the corner of Ataülf and Gignàs Street has been here since the late 18th century. It was, as it says on the façade, a *botica de la Corona*, a royal supplier. The pharmacist José Antonio Balcells proved that soldiers in Napoleon's army, who at that time had control over Barcelona, had been poisoned with an arsenic derivative. It's a historical anecdote from 1812, known as the 'Poison Conspiracy'.

483 REMAINS OF THE 1428 EARTHQUAKE

C/ Sant Domènech 6
El Gòtic ②

This house is leaning forward, not because of a construction error but because of the 1428 earthquake, the biggest one to ever hit Catalonia. The building is the oldest one in the city.

484 BOMB SHELTER 307

C/ Nou de la
Rambla 175
Poble Sec/Montjuïc ⑥
+34 (0)93 256 21 00
www.museuhistoria.
bcn.cat

This Civil War bomb shelter, Refugi 307, consists of nearly 400 metres of tunnels. It was excavated by the population of the Poble Sec/Montjuïc district. It has a number of different rooms, including a toilet, a water fountain, an infirmary, a children's room and a fireplace.

485 REFUGI MIRADOR DEL CARMELO

C/ Marià Labèrnia s/n
Gràcia ⑪
+34 (0)93 256 21 22
museuhistoria.bcn.cat/
ca/node/371

The Turó de la Rovira heritage site has been open to visitors since 2011. It contains the remains of an anti-aircraft battery from the Civil War, as well as a small museum about the Civil War and about the huts and shacks that the locals used to live in until the 1950s. Shows a very different side of Barcelona.

5 compelling
URBAN LEGENDS

486 THE 33 SQUARE OF SAGRADA FAMILIA

C/ de Mallorca 401
Dret de l'Eixample ⑩

Entering the Sagrada Familia by the Passion Façade Gates, you'll notice a square, comprised of 16 boxes filled with numbers. The sum of all lines (horizontal, vertical and diagonal) equals 33. Since Gaudí was rumoured to be a freemason, many have related that number to the 33 degrees of initiation. However, the artwork isn't Gaudí's – it's by Josep Maria Subirachs, who designed this gate of the church – and the number 33 refers to Jesus' age when he died on the cross.

487 CARRER DEL BISBE BRIDGE

Carrer del Bisbe s/n
El Gòtic ②

This bridge across Carrer del Bisbe features a sculpture of a crossed skull. Urban legend has it the city will crumble if the dagger is removed. The bridge was only constructed in the 1920s, by architect Joan Rubió i Bellver, who wanted to turn the Gothic neighbourhood into a Gothic theme park. The project was shelved; for a consolation prize, Rubió i Bellver got to design the bridge.

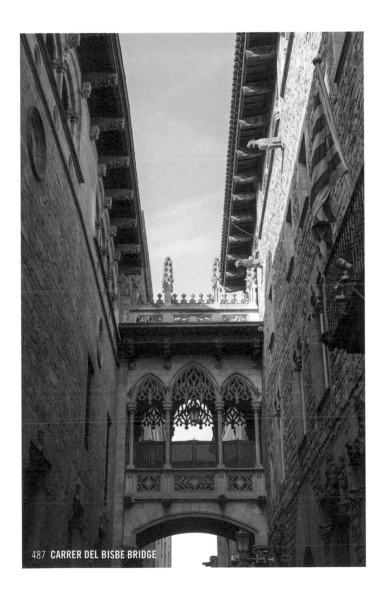

487 **CARRER DEL BISBE BRIDGE**

488 THE EXECUTIONER'S HOUSE

Plaça del Rei s/n
El Gòtic ②

Not a rich man, the city executioner lived in the narrowest house in Barcelona, now integrated in the Museu d'Història de Barcelona. Thanks to the balcony, the façade is still recognizable. Narrow as it was, the house had one advantage: it was right next to the executioner's workplace, the Plaça del Rei. According to rumours, the executioner made an extra buck selling the bones of the deceased, for use in potions and amulets.

489 MASONIC SUNDIAL

Parc de la Ciutadella
Born ③

The work of art at the park entrance closest to the França railway station, what is it exactly? It's a small column, a globe with roman numbers. According to some, it resembles the artwork at the entrance of masonic temples. In reality, it's a sundial, dating back to the 1888 World Fair.

490 ROCAFORT METRO STATION

Gran Via de les Corts Catalanes s/n
Eixample ⑨

Metro stations are the haunted houses of the 20th century. People have been seen waiting in Gaudì metrostation (which is not open to the public; see secret 471). Rocafort is supposedly haunted, with a record number of suicides, and cameras registering movement after closing time.

5 noteworthy
ODDITIES

---

491 THE CLOSED WINDOW OF THE PALAU DE LA ADUANA

Passeig de Josep
Carner 27
Barceloneta ④

Currently a government building, this 18th-century building is known as the Palau de la Aduana ('the Customs Palace'), named after its former occupants. The big windows with balconies all around are its most important feature, but one of them is permanently closed, even blocked from the inside, because once a detainee escaped through this window.

492 THE CATHEDRAL'S DOOR TO NOWHERE

Pla de la Seu s/n
El Gòtic ②
+34 (0)93 315 15 54
www.catedralbcn.org

If you look up to the Barcelona Cathedral on Plaça Sant Iu, you'll notice a useless, dark wooden door in the façade, about three storeys high. This is not God's personal exit, but the King's: on the other side of the street is the Palau Reial Major, a property of the crown, and a bridge across the street used to connect the palace with the Cathedral. The bridge was destroyed in 1714.

493 SNAIL HOUSE

Carrer de Tamarit 89
Sant Antoni ⑦

The façade of this house is decorated with dozens of snails. Look for the two bas-reliefs up high, which show how a man, earning a living by catching and selling snails, happens upon a cauldron of gold coins, in a cave on nearby Montjuïc. Why the owners wanted all those snails is a secret architect Carles Bosch Negre took to the grave.

494 THE BAILÈN TEMPLE

Carrer de Bailèn 72
Dret de l'Eixample ⑩

So what's up with that strange temple, a mixture of Roman temple and modernist touches, in Carrer de Bailèn? It was built in the late 19th century for the Masriera brothers. They were jewellers and the toast of the town. Nowadays, elderly nuns live here. The gates are permanently closed and the garden is growing into a further barrier between the temple and the world.

495 THE PAVILLION BEHIND Z-6

Plaça Carles Buigas
Poble Sec/Montjuïc ⑥

When everything was ready for the 1929 World Fair and every visiting country had gotten its own pavilion, the city realized it had forgotten to build one for the Spanish King. The Pabellón de la Ciudad was built in three months and is still quite beautiful. The pavilion is now almost behind a storage facility called hangar Z-6.

5 *reasons to*

LOOK UP

---

496 THE OWL

Avinguda Diagonal/
Passeig de Sant Joan
Dret de l'Eixample ⑩

Barcelona is a tall city: it pays to look up, once in a while. Even on a bland, traffic-heavy street like Avinguda Diagonal you might get surprised. The owl on top of that building should have disappeared a long time ago: the company it advertised for doesn't exist anymore and the use of neon at night became forbidden. But the people liked it, so now the owl is just an owl, no publicity, no neon. It overlooks with stern annoyance the hustle and bustle below.

497 LA CASA DE LAS PARAGUAS

Les Rambles 82
Raval ①

Casa Bruno Quadros is better known as the 'House of the Umbrellas'. There was an umbrella shop on the ground floor, when architect Josep Vilaseca started renovating the house in 1883, riding the first wave of modernist creations. The building doesn't just show umbrellas, there are also oriental elements, including a large forged-iron dragon jutting out of the corner.

496 **THE OWL**

498 TORRE DEL RELOJ

Moll dels
Pescadors s/n
Barceloneta ④

An overlooked Barceloneta beauty, the Clock Tower used to be a lighthouse, when this part of the beach was still used as a commercial harbour. When the lighthouse became obsolete, a clock was installed in the top.

499 TORRE DE LES AIGÜES DEL BESÒS

Plaça de Ramon
Calsina
Poblenou ⑤
+34 (0)93 256 36 42

This one isn't overlooked but overshadowed: by nearby Torre Agbar. This water tower is one of the last remains of Poblenou's industrial past and can be visited.

500 POST OFFICE BUILDING DOME

Via Laietana 1
Barceloneta ④

The central post office building is a mastodont on the outside and inside it looks like the perfect place to shoot a Franz Kafka movie adaptation. Take a ticket and while you are waiting to buy some stamps for your postcards, look up towards the glass dome, the semi-Graeco-Roman murals and (a bit lower) the guilded lanterns. In the vestibule are two antique bikes, used by the Spanish postal services to deliver mail and telegrams.

INDEX

COLOPHON

EDITING *and* COMPOSING — Mark Cloostermans
GRAPHIC DESIGN — Joke Gossé
PHOTOGRAPHY — Tino van den Berg - www.autoexilio.com
COVER IMAGE — Palau de la Música

The addresses in this book have been selected after thorough independent research by the author, in collaboration with Luster Publishers. The selection is solely based on personal evaluation of the business by the author. Nothing in this book was published in exchange for payment or benefits of any kind.

D/2016/12.005/2
ISBN 978 94 6058 1748
NUR 506

© 2016, Luster, Antwerp
Third edition, June 2017
www.lusterweb.com – www.the500hiddensecrets.com
info@lusterweb.com

Printed in Italy by Printer Trento.

MIX
Paper from
responsible sources
FSC® C015829
www.fsc.org